WHAT IS AMERICA EATING?

PROCEEDINGS OF A SYMPOSIUM

Food and Nutrition Board
Commission on Life Sciences
National Research Council

NATIONAL ACADEMY PRESS
Washington, D.C. 1986

National Academy Press   2101 Constitution Avenue, NW   Washington, DC 20418

The work on which this publication is based was supported by the National Research Council Fund—a pool of private, discretionary, nonfederal funds that is used to support a program of Academy-initiated studies of national issues in which science and technology figure significantly. The Fund consists of contributions from a consortium of private foundations including the Carnegie Corporation of New York, the Charles E. Culpeper Foundation, the William and Flora Hewlett Foundation, the John D. and Catherine T. MacArthur Foundation, the Andrew W. Mellon Foundation, the Rockefeller Foundation, and the Alfred P. Sloan Foundation; the Academy Industry Program, which seeks annual contributions from companies that are concerned with the health of U.S. science and technology and with public policy issues with technological content; and the National Academy of Sciences and the National Academy of Engineering endowments.

Food and Nutrition Board

iii

Preface

Each year, the Food and Nutrition Board (FNB) sponsors a symposium to stimulate discussion among scientists, practitioners, policymakers, and the public on a topic of particular interest to the nutrition community. A symposium entitled "What is America Eating?" was held December 10, 1984, at the National Academy of Sciences in Washington, D.C.

Selecting a topic for the 1984 symposium was particularly difficult because many issues in nutrition—both in the United States and abroad—deserved special attention. For example, the widespread starvation and malnutrition in developing countries such as Ethiopia would have been a topic of timely and global significance. The implications of developments in genetic engineering for our food supply are also of widespread interest. Another topic, nutrition monitoring in the United States, has been in the forefront of nutrition discussions among scientists, the U.S. Congress, and federal agencies, especially the U.S. Department of Agriculture (USDA) and the U.S. Department of Health and Human Services (DHHS)—agencies that have the primary responsibility for nutrition surveillance of the U.S. population. In Congress, discussions concerning the status and adequacy of federal nutrition-monitoring efforts have led to proposed legislation. In addition, at the request of USDA and DHHS, an FNB committee prepared a report on the uses and implications of USDA's Nationwide Food Consumption Survey and the dietary intake portion of the National Health and Nutrition Examination Survey, which is conducted by the National Center for Health Statistics.

From among all the critical nutrition-related topics deserving attention, the FNB selected the dietary habits of Americans—their trends, determinants, and nutritional consequences—as an outgrowth of its interest in nutrition surveillance. This challenging topic was greeted with enthusiasm by the speakers invited to participate in the symposium. As a result, their presentations were thoughtful, stimulating, and well received by all in attendance.

The FNB is a unit of the National Research Council's Commission on Life Sciences. It was established more than four decades ago, primarily to address issues of national importance that pertain to the safety and adequacy of the nation's food supply, to establish principles and guidelines for adequate nutrition, and to render authoritative judgment on the relationship between food intake, nutrition, and health. The FNB is a multidisciplinary group of biomedical scientists with expertise in various aspects of nutrition, food science, epidemiology, food toxicology, and food safety. These scientists deliberate on global issues concerning food and nutrition, initiate studies that are later assigned to standing or ad hoc FNB committees, and oversee the work of these committees.

The Food and Nutrition Board acknowledges Drs. Helen Guthrie, Jean-Pierre Habicht, Henry Kamin, and Stanley Johnson for their leadership in the planning of the symposium. The board is also grateful to Shirley Ash and Susan Barron for managing the arrangements for the symposium. Thanks are also due to Frances Peter and Judith Grumstrup-Scott for editing the proceedings.

Kurt Isselbacher, *Chairman*
Food and Nutrition Board

Contents

vii

WHAT IS AMERICA EATING?

Introduction

What are Americans eating? How are their current eating habits different from those a decade or two ago? In what ways are we monitoring these trends? Do these trends have significance for human health? What factors influence food selection? How do nutrition programs and public policy affect the diets of Americans? These questions and others were prominent in discussions of the Food and Nutrition Board (FNB) during the planning of the symposium whose proceedings appear in this volume.

The FNB was aware that it selected a complex topic for its 1984 annual symposium and that there are a variety of explanations for dietary habits, depending on one's perspective or expertise. Nonetheless, it concluded that the subject should be confronted because of the enormous interest of the general public in food for its own sake and for its beneficial and adverse effects on health. Never before has there been such a proliferation of books, specialty food stores, and feature articles on food in magazines and newspapers—from recipes to weight reduction plans and advice on nutrition and health. The strong market for these products points to the unparalleled fascination of Americans with the food they eat. No longer are they content with the straightforward turn-of-the-century diet consumed in most American homes and restaurants, but instead their interest has diversified to include the cuisines of many nations and specialized diets intended to promote health. Along with this diversification, there has been an exponential growth of the fast food business. As more women have left the traditional role of housekeeper and cook for the business world, the availability of palatable, inexpensive, and easily obtainable

1

food has become more and more attractive, giving rise to construction of the hamburger- and fried chicken-dispensing facilities that line our highways today. Both the exotic and more mundane diets can be either a short-term fad or a long-term commitment. Thus, their nutritional consequences must be carefully monitored and analyzed.

Legislators have also been interested in the nutritional needs of Americans. They have been actively studying the adequacy of federal nutrition-monitoring efforts and have recently proposed legislation (H.R. 2436) in an attempt to coordinate nutrition surveillance efforts of the U.S. Department of Agriculture (USDA) and the U.S. Department of Health and Human Services (DHHS).

The federal agencies and the scientific community have long been examining the food habits of Americans. Contributions to the understanding of this important subject have been made not only by investigators in the field of nutrition but also by experts in physiology, psychology, economics, and consumer behavior. Thus, the scope of the symposium was expanded to include these perspectives as all-important components of the overall subject.

Although the stimulus for this symposium was provided by interest in nutrition monitoring, the speakers were not asked to address the adequacy of nutrition surveillance. Rather, they focused on what the major food consumption surveys and other large-scale studies have demonstrated about food consumption patterns in the United States along with the determinants, trends, and consequences of food selection. The program was divided into four major sessions to accommodate these concerns. This organization is represented by four parallel sections in this volume.

In the first section, entitled "Eating Patterns, Nutrition, and Health in the United States," the symposium participants review data on eating patterns over the past two decades based on information from the two major surveys conducted by USDA and DHHS. The implications of this knowledge for nutrition and the health status of the U.S. population are also discussed. This subject will be covered in depth in a soon-to-be completed report of the Joint Nutrition Monitoring Evaluation Committee, whose mandate is briefly described.

The second section is entitled "What Factors Shape Eating Patterns?" Approaches to understanding the motivations for food choices and eating patterns are presented by a psychologist, an economist, and a consumer behaviorist.

"Eating Trends and Nutritional Consequences" is the title of the third section, which is devoted to eating trends and their implications for nutrition, with emphasis on socioeconomic groups that are at nutritional risk.

Certain trends in food choice are believed to have important effects on nutritional status.

The fourth section is an integrative presentation entitled ''Perspectives on Nutrition Programs, Policy, and Research.'' Contributors to this section explore the roles of policymaking bodies and the food industry in nutrition research and in nutrition programs for monitoring public education.

I
Eating Patterns, Nutrition, and Health in the United States

The Joint Nutrition Monitoring Evaluation Committee

SUSAN WELSH

The Joint Nutrition Monitoring Evaluation Committee (JNMEC), established on October 11, 1983, is a federal advisory committee jointly sponsored by the U.S. Department of Agriculture (USDA) and the U.S. Department of Health and Human Services (DHHS). The committee's overall mission is to develop at 3-year intervals a series of reports, principally intended for Congress, on the nutritional status of the U.S. population. Data for these evaluations will be collected by the National Nutrition Monitoring System, and the committee will continue to function as long as it provides the best means of achieving its mission.

JNMEC FUNCTIONS

The primary function of the JNMEC, as stated in its charter, is to integrate and interpret information from the component parts of the National Nutrition Monitoring System and to draw conclusions regarding the nutritional status of the U.S. population. This assessment will include a detailed analysis of the nutritional health and dietary status of the general population, analyses of particular subgroups that appear to have nutritional problems or nutrition-related health problems, and discussion of the factors that may influence nutritional health and dietary status.

The secondary function of the JNMEC is to assess the adequacy of the National Nutrition Monitoring System. As the committee reviews the nutritional status of the U.S. population and the factors that influence it (its primary function), it will also identify deficiencies, discrepancies, or

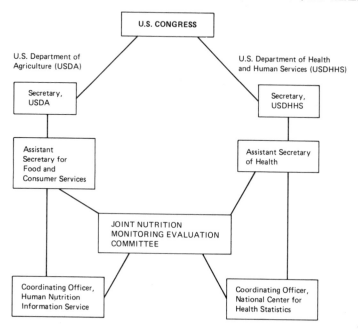

FIGURE 1   The Joint Nutrition Monitoring Evaluation Committee's organizational relationship with the U.S. Department of Agriculture and the U.S. Department of Health and Human Services.

unnecessary duplications in the monitoring system. The committee will apprise the USDA and DHHS of these problems and suggest methods for improvement.

JNMEC ORGANIZATION

The JNMEC's relationship to USDA and DHHS is shown in Figure 1. The committee members, four nongovernmental experts in nutrition or nutrition-related disciplines, are appointed for 2-year terms by the Assistant Secretary for Food and Consumer Services, USDA, and the Assistant Secretary for Health, DHHS, who jointly chair the committee. Both departments provide staff support. The USDA Human Nutrition Information Service (HNIS) provides an official to act as Executive Secretary of the committee and to coordinate the provision of information from USDA's nutrition-monitoring efforts. The DHHS National Center for Health Statistics (NCHS) provides an official to assist in fulfilling the responsibilities of the secretariat and to coordinate the provision of information from DHHS's nutrition-monitoring efforts.

During its first year of existence, the committee was cochaired by USDA's Assistant Secretary for Food and Consumer Service, Mary C. Jarratt, and by DHHS's Assistant Secretary for Health, Edward N. Brandt, Jr.[1]

The duties of the JNMEC members are solely advisory. The USDA and DHHS staffs provide to the committee information from department-conducted surveys and studies. Following its evaluation of this information, the committee will report, through the USDA Assistant Secretary for Food and Consumer Services and the DHHS Assistant Secretary for Health, to the Secretary of Agriculture and the Secretary of Health and Human Services. The appropriate USDA and DHHS clearance channels will be used. When final, the reports will be issued jointly by USDA and DHHS to Congress.

Fiscal and administrative support for the JNMEC was assumed within existing USDA and DHHS programs. No additional resources were allotted to USDA or DHHS for support of the JNMEC. Nongovernmental committee members serve without pay, and USDA and DHHS share committee members' travel expenses and costs of publishing and distributing reports. (For the first report, USDA will pay travel expenses and DHHS will pay publication costs.)

HISTORY OF THE JNMEC

The Food and Agriculture Act (U.S. Code, 1977) instructed the Secretary of Agriculture and the Secretary of Health, Education, and Welfare (HEW) (now Health and Human Services) to submit to Congress a proposal for a comprehensive nutrition status monitoring system that would integrate the ongoing nutrition survey activities of both departments. The original proposal, entitled "A Comprehensive Nutritional Status Monitoring System" (USDA and DHEW, 1978), acknowledged deficiencies and recommended improvement and expansion of the existing system. The proposal was an important working document for USDA and DHEW, prompting the establishment of various coordinating mechanisms, both formal and informal, for identifying and managing common areas of concern.

---

[1]The committee members were Helen A. Guthrie, Professor of Nutrition, Pennsylvania State University; Jean-Pierre Habicht, Professor of Nutrition, Cornell University; Stanley R. Johnson, Professor of Economics, Iowa State University; and Theodore B. Van Itallie, Professor of Medicine, Columbia University at St. Luke's Roosevelt Hospital Center. Advisors to the committee were Robert L. Rizek, HNIS, USDA, and Robert S. Murphy, NCHS, DHHS. DHHS staff support to the committee was coordinated by Catherine E. Woteki, NCHS, DHHS. USDA staff support was coordinated by Susan Welsh, who also served as Executive Secretary.

Following submission of the proposal to Congress, the Committee on Science and Technology requested that the General Accounting Office (GAO) review the proposal. Subsequently, GAO (1978) recommended the development of a comprehensive implementation plan, and the House and Senate of the U.S. Congress also instructed USDA and DHHS to proceed with the plan.

Implementation Plan

USDA and DHHS submitted the Joint Implementation Plan for a Comprehensive National Nutrition Monitoring System to Congress in 1981 (USDA and DHHS, 1981). This plan integrated the nutrition-monitoring goals of USDA and DHHS, explained how USDA's and DHHS's separate nutrition-monitoring activities fit together to form a comprehensive monitoring system, and set specific objectives for improving the system.

Goals and Objectives.   The goals of the National Nutrition Monitoring System, as set forth in the Joint Implementation Plan, were:

• to provide the scientific foundation for the maintenance and improvement of the nutritional status of the U.S. population and of the nutritional quality and healthfulness of the national food supply;
• to collect, analyze, and disseminate timely data on the nutritional and dietary status of the U.S. population, the nutritional quality of the food supply, food consumption patterns, and consumer knowledge and attitudes concerning nutrition;
• to identify high-risk groups of individuals and geographic areas, as well as nutrition-related problems and trends, in order to facilitate prompt implementation of nutrition intervention activities;
• to establish national baseline data for the National Nutrition Monitoring System and to develop and improve uniform standard methods, criteria, policies, and procedures for nutrition monitoring; and
• to provide data for evaluating changes in agricultural policy related to food production, processing, and distribution that may affect the nutritional quality and healthfulness of the U.S. food supply.

To achieve these goals, nutrition monitoring includes a variety of measurement activities that assess periodically and systematically the health and dietary status of the American people and the factors that may influence health and dietary status. Thus, comprehensive nutrition monitoring is not one simple task, but a complex and interconnected set of measurements.

The objectives presented in the Implementation Plan had as their intended result the integration of existing components of the nutrition-monitoring system to form a truly operational, comprehensive monitoring system. The first objective was that USDA and DHHS achieve the best possible coordination between the two largest and most important components of the system: the Nationwide Food Consumption Survey (NFCS) and the National Health and Nutrition Examination Survey (NHANES). Several specific activities were outlined, the completion of which would greatly improve the coordination of the surveys.

The second major objective of the Implementation Plan was the establishment of the JNMEC, a committee that would function as an evaluation and reporting mechanism for the National Nutrition Monitoring System. The USDA Assistant Secretary for Food and Consumer Services and the DHHS Assistant Secretary for Health solicited members for the committee in June 1982. USDA and DHHS prepared the committee's charter and, to comply with the Federal Advisory Committee Act (U.S. Code, 1972), submitted it for review by the General Services Administration and the Office of Management and Budget and published it in the *Federal Register* (USDA, 1983) for public comment. The committee was officially established in the fall of 1983; six meetings were held during the first year, and all were open to the public with prior announcement in the *Federal Register*.

November 1984 was proposed in the Implementation Plan as a target date for the first report. Despite the diligence of the committee and the commitment of USDA and DHHS, the less than 1 year of preparation time was not sufficient. The committee and the departments are concerned that the first report on the nutritional status of the U.S. population set the proper precedent for future reports. Therefore, the first report is scheduled to be completed late in 1985.

FIRST JNMEC REPORT

Because the JNMEC is a permanent national advisory committee and will publish reports periodically, the members decided that their first report should focus on baseline, descriptive information on which subsequent reports might build. The information available to the committee for this report includes data collected by the National Nutrition Monitoring System, a complex, interconnected set of measurements that comprise five major categories:

- health status measurements
- food consumption measurements
- food composition measurements
- dietary knowledge and attitude assessments
- food supply determinations

Measurements of health status and food consumption are the primary nutrition-monitoring activities, and information gathered through such efforts will be the major focus of the first report. Implicit in these two categories are all related research activities on human dietary needs, survey methodology, physiological measures, biochemical analyses, and standards for assessing dietary and health data.

Food composition measurements can be used to convert food consumption measurements into information about dietary levels of nutrients, which also may be related to health status measurements. In addition, food composition data are necessary for dietary planning and guidance. All the research necessary for the development of food composition data is implicit in this category.

Assessments of nutrition knowledge and attitudes concerning foods provide information on some of the factors that may influence nutritional status and also provide important clues to the best methods for improving nutritional status. This important aspect of nutrition monitoring will be briefly discussed in the first committee report.

Food supply determinations provide information on per capita quantities of food available for consumption since 1909. The assessment of trends in the levels of nutrients and other food components in the food supply is an important part of evaluating the nutritional status of Americans and will be included in the first committee report. Other activities that might be classified under one of the five major categories include regular determinations of food retail sales patterns and results from special evaluations of food programs, such as the Food Stamp Program and the School Lunch Program.

Data Sources

The primary data sources for the first committee report are the NFCS and NHANES. These two surveys are the cornerstones of the National Nutrition Monitoring System: Their sample sizes are large relative to other federal nutrition-monitoring efforts, and they provide representative pictures of diets and major public health problems in the United States.

NFCS. The most recent NFCS was conducted by the USDA's Human Nutrition Information Service (HNIS) in 1977-1978.[2] A national proba-

---

[2]Information about the NFCS and other USDA nutrition-monitoring activities has been published. For specific citations, write to the U.S. Department of Agriculture, Human Nutrition Information Service, Federal Building, Room 325-A, Hyattsville, MD 20782.

bility sample of U.S. households was surveyed, and information was collected both on the food used at home by the entire household and on food eaten at home and away from home by individual household members. Included were the kinds, amounts, and costs of foods brought into a household during a 7-day period and foods actually ingested by household members during a 3-day period. Data also were collected on numerous socioeconomic variables, such as income, education, and participation in food assistance programs; on source of food and eating occasion; and on household members' self-assessment of their diets and health.

Beginning in 1935, USDA conducted similar surveys at roughly 10-year intervals. In the first four surveys, information was collected on household food use only. In the last two surveys, information was also collected on the diets of individual household members. In the 1965-1966 survey, 1-day dietary recalls were collected from household members, and in 1977-1978, dietary recall was extended to 3 days.

NHANES. The NHANES is conducted periodically by the NCHS.[3] In this monitoring activity, representative samples of the U.S. population are surveyed and data are collected from health histories, physical examinations, various body measurements and biochemical analyses, and a 24-hour dietary recall and food frequency questionnaire. Two surveys have been completed: HANES I, conducted between 1971 and 1974, and NHANES II, conducted between 1976 and 1980. A Hispanic Health and Nutrition Examination Survey was conducted between 1982 and 1984.

Other Activities. In addition to the NFCS and NHANES, both USDA and DHHS have other nutrition-monitoring activities. For example, USDA's HNIS maintains the historical series of the nutrient content of the U.S. food supply as well as the National Nutrient Data Bank—a computerized source of food composition data. In its five nutrition research centers, USDA's Agricultural Research Service conducts basic research on human nutritional requirements and methods for determining food composition. In some states, DHHS's Centers for Disease Control collect information on the health status of persons using public health facilities. The Total Diet Study conducted by DHHS's Food and Drug Administration (FDA) determines levels of selected nutrients and contaminants in diets prepared from standard market baskets of foods in several regions of the country. The FDA and the USDA's Economic Research Service collect

---

[3]Information about the NHANES and other DHHS nutrition-monitoring activities has been published. For specific citations write to Scientific and Technical Information Branch, National Center for Health Statistics, Public Health Service, Hyattsville, MD 20782.

information on the public's knowledge and attitudes concerning food. Other DHHS activities include natality and mortality statistics. Both USDA and DHHS conduct research on methods and standards for nutritional assessment.

The quantity and quality of dietary and health data available to the committee for their first report varied among food components and related health conditions. The availability of standards for evaluating the data and the ease of interpreting the data also varied. Table 1 shows the relative completeness of dietary and health data from the major sources of information used in the report. Food components not listed in Table 1 will not be included in the first JNMEC report because available data were not considered sufficient.

PROGRESS

USDA and DHHS have made progress toward the goals of the National Nutrition Monitoring System as set forth in the Joint Implementation Plan. It is anticipated that the quantity and quality of dietary and health data and the ease of interpretation will change considerably in the years to come as a result of current research efforts.

NFCS and NHANES

Two important activities that have led to better coordination between the most important components of the National Nutrition Monitoring System—the NFCS and the NHANES—began in 1977. At that time, USDA and DHHS formed the Working Group on Surveys of Food Consumption, Nutrition, and Health and initiated work on the National Nutrition Monitoring System. In 1981, USDA and DHHS appointed a committee of statisticians to study coordination of NFCS and NHANES, and in September 1982, 9 months after its appointment, the NFCS-NHANES Coordination Committee completed its work. Their recommendations for the future, which are currently being implemented, include (1) use of the same coding system; (2) coordination of questions and interviewer instructions and training; (3) use of compatible nutrient data base, sex and age categories, and standards for analyzing data; and (4) use of sampling plans that will ensure the comparability of the data.

Under a grant from USDA and DHHS, the Food and Nutrition Board (FNB) of the National Research Council recently published a report on the priority uses of national survey data on food consumption (NRC, 1984). USDA and DHHS are taking into consideration the findings of this study, including the recommendations for more effective means of obtaining data, in planning USDA and DHHS surveys.

Methodology Studies

Studies in which various methods of survey data collection are tested and that ultimately result in improved data are an important part of the research programs of USDA and DHHS. In 1982, USDA began two major pilot studies necessary for the development of a continuous survey methodology. One study included tests of nine alternative procedures for collecting intake data from persons for up to 12 days over a 1-year period. Data were collected by personal interview, telephone, mail, and combinations of these methods. The second was a pilot study of these procedures with selected low-income populations. Some findings from these studies have already been incorporated in plans for future surveys, but analyses of all results have not been completed.

Other methodology studies have been recently completed or are in progress at several universities under agreements with USDA. For example, the effect of some of the methodological differences between USDA and DHHS surveys have been studied. Methods for improving the dietary recall process have also been analyzed. In some studies, household food discard and food frequency were measured, and the use of food models and other quantity guides was determined. The association of diet with economic factors is also being studied. In an administrative report now being planned, the results from recent methodological studies conducted by USDA will be summarized.

Nutritional Status Standards

One of the difficulties encountered by USDA and DHHS has been the availability of appropriate standards for the assessment of nutritional status from dietary and health data. The nutrient levels of diets reported in surveys are usually compared to the FNB's Recommended Dietary Allowances (RDA) (NRC, 1980). The nutrient needs of almost all healthy people are met by diets that provide the RDA, but the degree of risk associated with nutrient intakes below the RDA is uncertain. A special committee established by the FNB and funded by a grant from USDA is examining the methodology for assessing such risks. The committee's report is scheduled for release in late 1985.

TABLE 1 Summary of Food Components Classified by the Completeness of Available Data[a]

Data Completeness and Food Component	Dietary Data				Health Data			
	Source of Data				Source of Data			
	U.S. Food Supply Series	NFCS		Criteria for Assessment[b]	NHANES	CDC Surveillance		Criteria for Assessment[c]
		Household	Individual			Pediatric	Pregnant	
Most complete								
Food energy	*	*	*	*	*	*		*
Protein	*	*	*	*	*			*
Vitamin A	*	*	*	*	*			*
Vitamin C	*	*	*	*	*			*
Iron	*	*	*	*	*	*	*	*
Less complete								
Thiamin	*	*	*	*				
Riboflavin	*	*	*	*				
Niacin	*	*[d]	*	*				
Vitamin B$_6$	*	*[d]	*[d]	*	*			*
Vitamin B$_{12}$	*	*[d]	*[d]	*				
Calcium	*	*	*	*				
Phosphorus	*	*	*	*				

TABLE 1 Continued

Data Completeness and Food Component	Dietary Data — Source of Data — U.S. Food Supply Series	NFCS Household	NFCS Individual	Criteria for Assessment[b]	Health Data — Source of Data — NHANES	CDC Surveillance Pediatric	CDC Surveillance Pregnant	Criteria for Assessment[c]
Least complete								
Folacin	*			*	*			*
Magnesium	*	*d	*d	*				
Sodium	*		*d	*				
Zinc	*			*	*			*e
Fat	*	*	*					
Fatty acids	*							
Cholesterol	*		*d		*			*
Carbohydrate	*	*	*d					
Added sweeteners	*		*d					
Crude fiber	*							
Alcoholic beverages	*f							*

aFrom U.S. food supply series, 1909–1982; NFCS, Nationwide Food Consumption Survey, 1955, 1965, and 1977–1978 (household data only for 1955); NHANES, National Health and Nutrition Examination Surveys, 1976–1980; CDC, Centers for Disease Control surveillance data, 1975–1983.
bRecommended Dietary Allowances (NRC, 1980).
cGenerally accepted physiological and biochemical criteria.
dFood composition data or criteria were less reliable for these nutrients than for others in 1977–1978.
eStandards for assessing health data on zinc are less certain than standards for other food components.
fData from DHHS, 1981.

Health Status

The availability and ease of interpreting physiological and biochemical measures of nutritional status also vary. Some measures, e.g., body weight and height, are obtained and interpreted relatively easily and inexpensively. Although several available clinical tests of iron nutrition vary in complexity and cost, their interpretation is difficult. For vitamin B_6, there are no simple tests of nutritional status, and for many of the trace elements, what should be measured as a test of adequate nutrition is not now known. The prevalence of certain diseases, such as hypertension or diabetes, is easier to measure than the prevalence of other diseases, such as atherosclerosis or osteoporosis—especially in the early stages of development.

The FDA has devoted considerable resources to the analysis of data collected in the NHANES program. Three reports have assessed nutritional status related to folacin, iron, and zinc (FASEB, 1984a,b,c). DHHS is also planning a Surgeon General's report on nutrition for 1986; this report will focus on the relationship between nutrition and disease.

Nutrient Composition of Foods

Since the last nationwide surveys by USDA and DHHS, information on food composition has increased considerably. In 1977-1978, the nutrient data base for approximately 4,000 food items contained values for energy and 14 nutrients: protein, fat, carbohydrate, calcium, iron, magnesium, phosphorus, vitamin A value (IU), thiamin, riboflavin, niacin, vitamin B_6, vitamin B_{12}, and vitamin C. Since then, USDA's computerized National Nutrient Data Bank has become fully operational, and the following additional nutrients and food components will be added to the data base: sodium, potassium, zinc, copper, folacin, cholesterol, total saturated fatty acids, total monounsaturated fatty acids, total polyunsaturated fatty acids, vitamin A as retinol equivalents, carotene as retinol equivalents, alpha-tocopherol equivalents, dietary fiber, and alcohol.

Future Surveys

Four major nutrition surveys are in various stages of progress or planning. Data collection for DHHS's Hispanic Health and Nutrition Examination Survey was completed in December 1984. This is the first large-scale survey of an ethnic group believed to be at nutritional risk. Plans for DHHS's third NHANES have been initiated, and it is scheduled to begin in 1988.

The Continuing Survey of Food Intakes by Individuals (CSFII), a major new thrust of USDA's monitoring efforts, began in April 1985. This continuing food consumption survey, which is the first nationwide dietary survey to be conducted yearly in the United States, was recommended in the Joint Implementation Plan (USDA and DHHS, 1981) and in the Research Council's report on the uses of food consumption data (NRC, 1984). The survey's objective is to measure the food and nutrient content of U.S. diets over time, to signal changes in food and nutrient intake, and to provide certain other information pertinent to evaluations of nutritional status. It will complement the decennial NFCS by providing continuous data on the dietary status of selected population subgroups, especially those who may be at nutritional risk. The ability to observe trends and anticipate potential problems from the results of the surveys will allow policymakers to formulate sound policies and programs with respect to agriculture, food assistance, nutrition education, and food fortification.

For the first year of the CSFII, the core-monitoring group will consist of women aged 19 to 50 years and their children aged 1 to 5 years in nationally representative samples of all income groups and of low-income groups. Six days of dietary data will be collected on each participant. Women were selected for the core-monitoring group because they are generally household food managers who know most about the food eaten— for example, how it was prepared and the kinds and amounts of ingredients. Also, women of childbearing age and young children were among the sex-age categories in the 1977-1978 survey with food intakes that most often failed to provide recommended amounts of nutrients. One day of dietary data will also be collected on a nationally representative sample of males 19 to 50 years of age. Other population subgroups considered to be at nutritional risk may be included in future surveys.

USDA's comprehensive decennial NFCS is planned for 1987. In this survey, comparable to NFCS 1977-1978, information will be collected on household food consumption and the monetary value of food as well as on 3-day food intakes of each household member. Nationally representative samples of households across all incomes and low-income households will be surveyed.

Both USDA and DHHS will strive to process the incoming data rapidly. Increased automation of the interview process is planned and under way, and standardized reporting formats that will facilitate comparisons of data from the NFCS and the NHANES will be developed.

CONCLUSIONS

Increases are anticipated in the quantity and quality of information obtained from the National Nutrition Monitoring System. The staffs of

USDA and DHHS are committed to this purpose and are working together to achieve common goals. As the amount of information from the component parts of the Monitoring System increases, the need for a reporting system to integrate and interpret the information will also increase. Efforts to meet this need will be aided by the work of the Joint Nutrition Monitoring Evaluation Committee.

REFERENCES

FASEB (Federation of American Societies for Experimental Biology). 1984a. Assessment of the Folate Nutritional Status of the U.S. Population Based on Data Collected in the Second National Health and Nutrition Examination Survey, 1976-1980. Life Sciences Research Office. FASEB Special Publications Office, Bethesda, Md.

FASEB (Federation of American Societies for Experimental Biology). 1984b. Assessment of the Iron Nutritional Status of the U.S. Population Based on Data Collected in the Second National Health and Nutrition Examination Survey, 1976-1980. Life Sciences Research Office. FASEB Special Publications Office, Bethesda, Md.

FASEB (Federation of American Societies for Experimental Biology). 1984c. Assessment of the Zinc Nutritional Status of the U.S. Population Based on Data Collected in the Second National Health and Nutrition Examination Survey, 1976-1980. Life Sciences Research Office. FASEB Special Publications Office, Bethesda, Md.

GAO (General Accounting Office). 1978. Future of the National Nutrition Intelligence System. Staff study, CED-79-5. General Accounting Office, Washington, D.C.

NRC (National Research Council). 1980. Recommended Dietary Allowances, 9th ed. A report of the Food and Nutrition Board, National Research Council. National Academy of Sciences, Washington, D.C.

NRC (National Research Council). 1984. National Survey Data on Food Consumption: Uses and Recommendations. A report of the Food and Nutrition Board, National Research Council. National Academy Press, Washington, D.C.

U.S. Code. 1972. Federal Advisory Committee Act. P.L. 92-463, 86 Stat. 770.

U.S. Code. 1977. Food and Agriculture Act of 1977. P.L. 95-113, 91 Stat. 913, Sect. 1428.

USDA (U.S. Department of Agriculture). 1983. Joint Nutrition Monitoring Evaluation Committee; Establishment. Fed. Regist. 48:38263-38264.

USDA and DHEW (U.S. Department of Agriculture and U.S. Department of Health, Education, and Welfare). 1978. Proposal—A Comprehensive Nutritional Status Monitoring System. Report submitted to U.S. Congress, March 6. Available from Human Nutrition Information Service, U.S. Department of Agriculture, Hyattsville, Md.

USDA and DHHS (U.S. Department of Agriculture and U.S. Department of Health and Human Services). 1981. Joint Implementation Plan for a Comprehensive National Nutrition Monitoring System. Report submitted to U.S. Congress. Available from Human Nutrition Information Service, U.S. Department of Agriculture, Hyattsville, Md.

DHHS (U.S. Department of Health and Human Services). 1981. Alcohol and Health. Fourth special report. National Institute on Alcoholism and Alcohol Abuse, National Institutes of Health, U.S. Department of Health and Human Services, Bethesda, Md.

Nutritional Status of the U.S. Population: Iron, Vitamin C, and Zinc

CATHERINE WOTEKI, CLIFFORD JOHNSON, and
ROBERT MURPHY

Conclusions can be drawn about the nutritional status of Americans by relating data on selected indicators of nutritional status to data on food consumption from two federal surveys: the second National Health and Nutrition Examination Survey (NHANES II), conducted by the Department of Health and Human Services (DHHS), and the Nationwide Food Consumption Survey (NFCS), conducted by the U.S. Department of Agriculture (USDA). In the first paper of this session, Dr. Welsh reviewed the sufficiency of nutrition-related data from the two most recent of these surveys. For some nutrients, a substantial quantity of data is available from both surveys. For other nutrients, data on dietary intake, on nutritional status, or on both may be of limited quantity or quality for a variety of reasons. To illustrate how conclusions about the nutritional status of Americans can be drawn from these surveys, three nutrients are discussed:

- iron, for which sufficient data are available to assess both nutritional status and dietary intake;
- vitamin C, for which there is only one indicator of nutritional status but sufficient dietary intake data; and
- zinc, for which there is one indicator of nutritional status and no data on dietary intake.

DATA SOURCES

The NHANES II was conducted by the DHHS National Center for Health Statistics from 1976 through 1980 on a national probability sample

21

of Americans aged 6 months through 74 years who were representative of the civilian, noninstitutionalized population (McDowell *et al.*, 1981). The results of this survey provide an opportunity to assess the U.S. population's health and nutritional status and, by comparing the data with results of earlier surveys, to learn how this status has changed over time. The NHANES II sample consisted of 27,801 persons from 64 geographical locations in the United States. Of these, 20,322 (73%) were interviewed and given a standardized physical examination. A detailed description of the survey design and its operations has been published in the Vital and Health Statistics Series of the National Center for Health Statistics (McDowell *et al.*, 1981).

The NFCS was conducted by the USDA Human Nutrition Information Service during 1977 and 1978 on a national probability sample of American households that were representative of the 48 coterminous states. It provides information on household food use over 7 days and household members' food and nutrient intakes over 3 days. The NFCS sample consisted of approximately 15,000 households and 36,000 persons residing in these households. Detailed descriptions of the household and individual surveys have been published (USDA, 1982, 1983).

IRON

Data from NHANES II

A primary focus of NHANES II was the characterization of the prevalence and possible cause of anemia in the U.S. population. To make this characterization, the survey team collected and analyzed blood specimens and reported values for hemoglobin, hematocrit, complete blood count, mean corpuscular volume, transferrin saturation, erythrocyte protoporphyrin, serum ferritin, serum vitamin B_{12}, serum folate, and erythrocyte folate.

In 1983, at the request of the Food and Drug Administration, the Federation of American Societies for Experimental Biology (FASEB) convened an expert Scientific Working Group (ESWG) to evaluate the appropriateness of the NHANES II measures and methods used, recommend interpretative criteria, estimate the prevalence of impaired iron status, and identify groups at greatest risk. Its report (FASEB, 1984a) is the source of the following discussion.

The ESWG developed two models based on four variables: serum ferritin, erythrocyte protoporphyrin, transferrin saturation, and mean corpuscular volume (MCV). The ferritin model is used to estimate early stages of iron store depletion and is based on measures of serum ferritin,

TABLE 1 Criteria Defining Abnormal Values of Four Measures of Iron Nutriture for Five Age Groups[a]

Age (year)	Serum Transferrin Ferritin (ng/ml)	Erythrocyte Saturation (%)	Protoporphyrin (μg/dl RBC[b])	MCV (fl)
1–2	NM[c]	<12	>80	<73
3–4	<10	<14	>75	<75
5–10	<10	<15	>70	<76
11–14	<10	<16	>70	<78
15–74	<12	<16	>70	<80

[a]Data from FASEB, 1984a.
[b]RBC, red blood cell.
[c]NM, not measured.

erythrocyte protoporphyrin, and transferrin saturation. The later stages of iron depletion are estimated with the MCV model, which is based on measures of mean corpuscular volume, erythrocyte protoporphyrin, and transferrin saturation. The criteria defining abnormal values for each variable are shown in Table 1. To be categorized as having impaired iron status, a person had to have at least two of three values in the abnormal range.

The prevalence estimates derived from the two models are shown in Figures 1, 2, and 3. Children aged 1 through 2 years had the highest

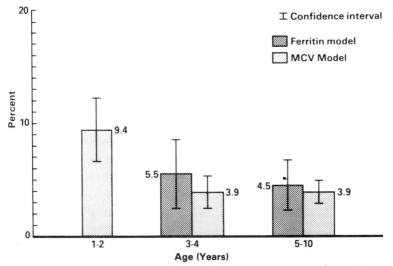

FIGURE 1 Prevalence of impaired iron status for American children aged 1 through 10 years, by model. Data from the second National Health and Nutrition Examination Survey (FASEB, 1984a).

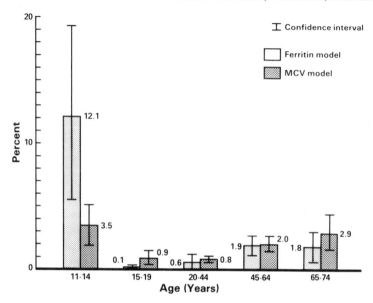

FIGURE 2   Prevalence of impaired iron status for American males aged 11 through 74 years, by model. Data from the second National Health and Nutrition Examination survey (FASEB, 1984a).

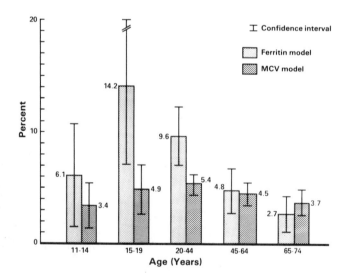

FIGURE 3   Prevalence of impaired iron status for American females aged 11 through 74 years, by model. Data from the second National Health and Nutrition Examination Survey (FASEB, 1984a).

prevalence of impaired iron status (9%) by the MCV model. Because serum ferritin was not measured in children in that age group, prevalence estimates using the ferritin model cannot be presented for those children. As expected, the ferritin model produced slightly higher prevalence estimates than did the MCV model for all sex and age groups. The groups with the highest prevalences were children aged 1 through 2 years, males aged 11 through 14 years, and females aged 15 through 44 years.

Data from NFCS

Dietary data from the NFCS (Welsh, 1984) indicate that the groups with the highest prevalences of impaired iron status had the lowest intakes of the Recommended Dietary Allowances (RDA) for iron (NRC, 1980). Children aged 1 through 8 years, males aged 9 through 18 years, and females aged 9 through 64 years had mean intakes below the RDA (Figure 4). About 37% of children aged 1 through 8 years and males aged 9 through 18 years of age consumed diets providing at least 100% of the RDA for iron over 3 days. The comparable figure for females aged 9 through 64 years was less than 20%.

These data indicate that the highest prevalence of impaired iron status

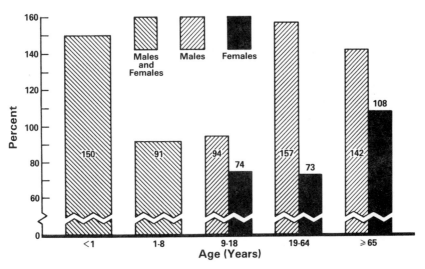

FIGURE 4 Individual intakes of iron: mean percentages of 1980 Recommended Dietary Allowances (RDAs), by sex and age (3-day average). Adapted from Welsh, 1984.

in the United States occurs in those groups with the lowest dietary intake of iron, expressed as a percentage of the RDA. However, the magnitude of the numbers is quite different. Although a substantial proportion of the U.S. population does not report diets containing the full RDA for iron, the overall prevalence of impaired iron status is low.

VITAMIN C

Assessments of vitamin C have been included in national surveys to determine the prevalence of scurvy and the proportion of the population at risk of deficiency. In recent years, interest in the vitamin C status of Americans has increased as evidence has accumulated for the role of the vitamin in inhibiting the formation of some carcinogens and for the association of the consumption of vitamin C-containing foods with a lower risk of stomach and esophageal cancer.

Data from NHANES II

By using data from NHANES II, one can identify and characterize subgroups of the population with low serum vitamin C. Diet, smoking habits, and other lifestyle factors that affect serum vitamin C levels can be examined. As part of the nutritional biochemistry assessments, serum vitamin C was to be analyzed for all persons aged 3 through 74 years as an indicator of vitamin C status. Of the 18,549 persons aged 3 through 74 years in the sample, however, the serum vitamin C values were recorded for only 15,796 (85%). The determinations were performed at the Centers for Disease Control using a modified colorimetric ascorbic acid method (Gunter et al., 1985).

Mean serum vitamin C levels differed by age and sex (Figure 5). For children, mean levels generally decreased with age from a high of about 1.5 mg/dl for the 3- through 5-year-old group to 1.1 mg/dl for the 15- through 17-year-old group. For adults, mean values remained fairly stable, although there was some increase in values for the older age group. Males had lower mean levels of serum vitamin C than did females for all the adult age categories.

The findings are reflected in the prevalence of low serum vitamin C levels in the surveyed population (Figure 6), where low was defined as less than 0.25 mg/dl. Very few children had low serum vitamin C levels. The prevalence of low values generally increased for teenagers, and adult males had a higher proportion of low values (5.6%) than did females (2.7%).

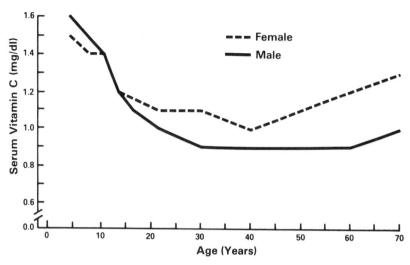

FIGURE 5 Mean serum vitamin C levels of Americans, by age and sex, 1976-1980. Unpublished data from the second National Health and Nutrition Examination Survey.

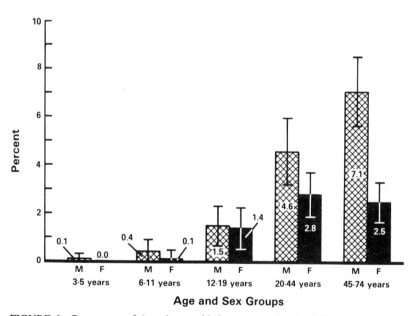

FIGURE 6 Percentage of Americans with low serum vitamin C levels, by age and sex, 1976-1980. Low serum vitamin C is defined as less than 0.25 mg/dl. Unpublished data from the second National Health and Nutrition Examination Survey.

Following is a list of the major variables generally believed to be associated with serum vitamin C status:

- age, sex, race
- poverty status
- vitamin-mineral supplement use (regular users as opposed to irregular or nonusers)
- cigarette smoking (current cigarette smokers; not pipe smokers, cigar smokers, or nonsmokers)
  - oral contraceptive use
  - dietary intake of vitamin C
  - frequency of consuming foods rich in vitamin C
  - fasting or nonfasting examination status
  - morning or afternoon examination
  - pregnancy status

Many of these characteristics were found to be significantly related to serum vitamin C.

Because of the relatively high percentage of low serum vitamin C levels in adults and because of differences between males and females, we characterized the population aged 20 through 74 years by cigarette-smoking status, dietary supplement use, and poverty status. Preliminary analysis of our data (Johnson *et al.*, 1984) had shown these factors to be associated with serum vitamin C levels.

The percentage of adults aged 20 through 44 years and 45 through 74 years in each of the cigarette-smoking and supplement use categories in the population are presented in Figure 7. The proportion of current cigarette smokers was higher in the younger adults. However, regular supplement use was highest in the 45- through 74-year-old age group. The percentage of the population in each of the categories was sufficient for more detailed analysis of the data.

Mean serum vitamin C levels were significantly higher for regular supplement users (1.3-1.5 mg/dl) than for irregular or nonusers (0.7-1.1 mg/dl) for both males and females in each cigarette-smoking category (Figure 8). With one exception, persons in the other smokers/nonsmokers group had higher mean serum vitamin C levels than did current cigarette smokers for each sex and supplement-use category.

These differences in smoking and supplement use categories for vitamin C status were even more pronounced when the prevalence of low serum vitamin C values (Figure 9) was considered. Males who used supplements regularly had prevalences less than 1%, regardless of their cigarette-smoking status. Irregular or nonusers of supplements had higher levels; 45- through

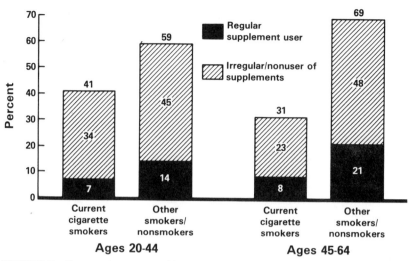

FIGURE 7   Current cigarette-smoking status and dietary supplement usage of Americans, by age group, measured as a percentage of the population, 1976-1980. Unpublished data from the second National Health and Nutrition Examination Survey.

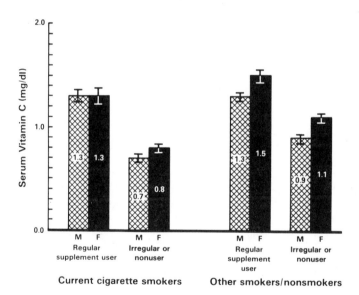

FIGURE 8   Mean serum vitamin C levels of Americans aged 21 through 74 years, by sex (pregnant women excluded), current cigarette-smoking status, and dietary supplement usage, 1976-1980. Unpublished data from the second National Health and Nutrition Examination Survey.

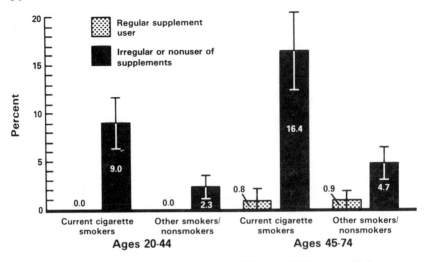

FIGURE 9   Percentage of American males aged 20 through 74 years with low serum vitamin C levels, by age group, current cigarette-smoking status, and dietary supplement usage, 1976-1980. Low serum vitamin C is defined as less than 0.25 mg/dl. Unpublished data from the second National Health and Nutrition Examination Survey.

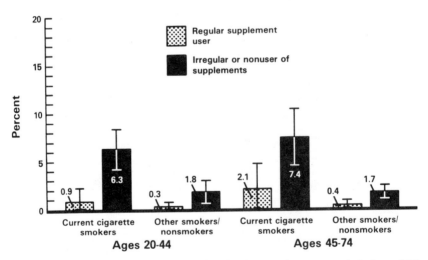

FIGURE 10   Percentage of American females (pregnant women excluded) aged 20 through 74 years with low serum vitamin C levels, by age group, current cigarette-smoking status, and dietary supplement usage, 1976-1980. Low serum vitamin C is defined as less than 0.25 mg/dl. Unpublished data from the second National Health and Nutrition Examination Survey.

74-year-old males who were current cigarette smokers had the highest prevalence (16.4%), followed by 20- through 44-year-old males (9%).

With one exception, we observed the same pattern for females as for males (Figure 10). The percentage of women with low serum vitamin C was low for all subpopulations that used supplements regularly. Only current cigarette smokers who did not use supplements regularly had a prevalence greater than 5%.

Because serum vitamin C reflects dietary intake, we used this measure to determine the vitamin C content of the diets of males and females classified by cigarette smoking and supplement use. Figure 11 shows that for median vitamin C intake based on a single 24-hour recall among males, regular supplement users had higher dietary levels than did irregular or nonusers within each age and smoking status category. Intakes by current cigarette smokers were lower than those for the other smoker/nonsmoker groups for all age and supplement use categories. Two groups had median vitamin C intakes below the 1980 RDA of 60 mg: the current cigarette smokers who were irregular or nonusers of supplements in both age groups.

Figure 12 shows a pattern for females similar to that observed in males. Within cigarette-smoking groups, the females aged 45 through 74 years had higher median intakes than did the younger adult women. The younger cigarette smokers and other smokers/nonsmokers not taking supplements had median intakes below the RDA of 60 mg.

The vitamin C density of the diets of male supplement users was higher than the median intakes of irregular or nonusers of supplements (Figure 13). We observed a similar pattern for females (Figure 14). We also compared the frequency with which fruits and vegetables high in vitamin C were consumed and found patterns similar to the median intake and intake per 1,000 kcal (Figures 13 and 14).

Although the overall percentage of 3- through 74-year-old persons with low serum vitamin C levels was not large (about 3%), this was not true for selected populations. There was a much higher percentage of low serum vitamin C values among cigarette-smoking adults who seldom or never used vitamin-mineral supplements than would be expected by their representation in the population. For males, 34% were current cigarette smokers who did not regularly use vitamin-mineral supplements. In this group, 71% of the men had low serum vitamin C. The comparable figures for women were 25% and 61%. In contrast, regular supplement users constituted approximately 20% of the male population, but less than 2% of the low serum vitamin C group. For women, regular supplement users constituted about 28% of the population and less than 8% of the low serum vitamin C group.

Because a smaller proportion of the low-income population reported regular

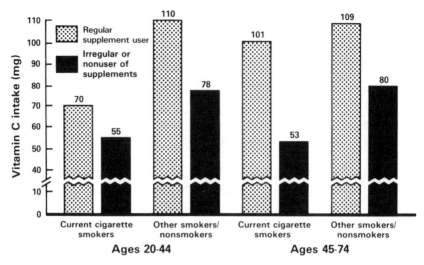

FIGURE 11   Median vitamin C intake of American males aged 20 through 74 years, by age group, current cigarette-smoking status, and dietary supplement usage, 1976-1980. Unpublished data from the second National Health and Nutrition Examination Survey.

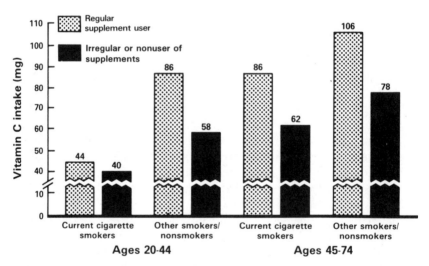

FIGURE 12   Mean vitamin C intake of American females (pregnant women excluded) aged 20 through 74 years, by age group, current cigarette-smoking status, and dietary supplement usage, 1976-1980. Unpublished data from the second National Health and Nutrition Examination Survey.

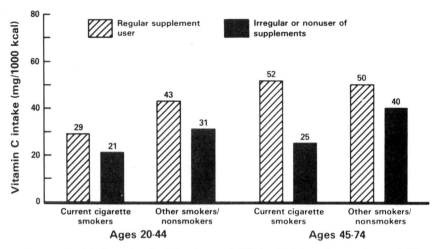

FIGURE 13   Median vitamin C intake per 1,000 kcal of American males aged 20 through 74 years, by age group, current cigarette-smoking status, and dietary supplement usage, 1976-1980. Unpublished data from the second National Health and Nutrition Examination Survey.

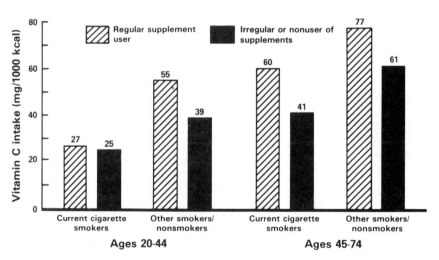

FIGURE 14   Median vitamin C intake per 1,000 kcal of American females aged 20 through 74 years (pregnant women excluded), by age group, current cigarette-smoking status, and dietary supplement usage, 1976-1980. Unpublished data from the second National Health and Nutrition Examination Survey.

use of vitamin-mineral supplements than did the general population, we determined the prevalence of low serum vitamin C by poverty status and supplement usage (Figure 15). The percentage of regular supplement users with low serum vitamin C levels was 1% or less, regardless of age, sex, or income. However, among irregular or nonsupplement users, those below poverty had higher prevalences of low serum vitamin C. Males aged 45 through 74 years had the highest prevalence of low values (24.2%).

A low serum vitamin C level indicates a low or inadequate intake of vitamin C, probably with low tissue reserves present. On the basis of this indicator, we have identified the following subpopulations with lifestyles that place them at high risk for poor vitamin C nutritional status:

● consumers of diets that are low in vitamin C because of infrequent consumption of vitamin C-rich foods and low vitamin C density of these diets,

  ● cigarette smokers,
  ● irregular or nonconsumers of vitamin or mineral supplements, and
  ● the poor.

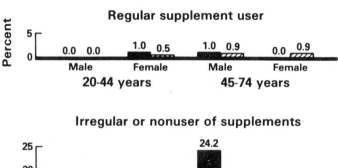

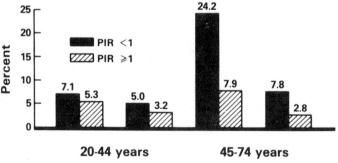

FIGURE 15   Prevalence of low serum vitamin C in the United States, by age, dietary supplement usage, and poverty income ratio (PIR), 1976-1980. Unpublished data from the second National Health and Nutrition Examination Survey.

Data from NFCS

Data on vitamin C from the NFCS indicate that mean intakes over 3 days exceeded the RDA for all sex and age groups (Table 2) and that mean intakes for men were higher than those for women aged 9 through 64 years. Those with a poverty income ratio (PIR) of 1 or more had higher mean intakes than those with a PIR of less than 1.

TABLE 2   Individual Intakes of Vitamin C, Measured as Mean Percentage of 1980 RDAs, by Selected Characteristics (3-Day Average), 1977–1978[a]

Category	Percentage of RDA
All persons:	147
Males and females:	
1 year	226
1–8 years	166
Males	
9–18 years	174
19–64 years	145
≥65 years	153
Females:	
9–18 years	152
19–64 years	128
≥65 years	150
Poverty status and race:	
Above poverty, white	149
Above poverty, black	152
Below poverty, white	125
Below poverty, black	138
Region:	
Northeast	160
North central	147
South	131
West	159
Urbanization:	
Central city	152
Suburban	153
Nonmetropolitan	136
Season:	
Spring	151
Summer	152
Fall	140
Winter	146

[a]Unpublished data from the Nationwide Food Consumption Survey.

Lifestyle variables, such as smoking habits and use of supplements, influence serum vitamin C, which is one measure of nutritional status. National dietary surveys have not provided the necessary information for survey analysts to calculate the nutrient contribution of supplements to daily intakes, and this information may not be available in the future because of the difficulty of maintaining a vitamin-mineral supplement composition data bank. Because 40% of the adult population is presently taking supplements (Gallup Organization, Inc., 1982), dietary intake alone is an inadequate predictor of serum vitamin C. What remains to be determined is whether a better measure of long-term vitamin C status will be developed and how it will relate to dietary survey results.

ZINC

Data from NHANES II

In NHANES II, serum zinc was measured by flame atomic absorption spectroscopy of serum samples obtained from 14,770 persons aged 3 through 74 years. Although at the time of the survey serum zinc was recognized as an inadequate measure for the definitive assessment of zinc nutritional status, the Centers for Disease Control wanted to test whether conditions could be maintained for trace element determinations in a large field survey. The ESWG, in which evaluations of iron nutriture were based on data from NHANES II, also made observations on zinc nutriture (FASEB, 1984b).

Because serum zinc values differ, depending on the time of blood collection and fasting, the ESWG recommended that different cutoff points be used to define low values for samples obtained in the morning for fasting and nonfasting persons and for afternoon and evening samples. These values are shown in Table 3.

TABLE 3 Cutoff Points Used to Define Low Serum Zinc Values for Samples Obtained at Different Times of Day and Fasting Conditions[a]

Time of Day	Fasting Status	Serum Zinc (μg/dl)
Morning	Fasting	70
Morning	Nonfasting	65
Afternoon and evening	Presumed fasting	60

[a]Data from FASEB, 1984b.

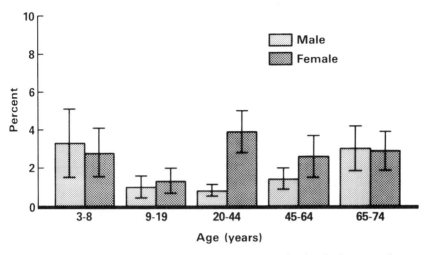

FIGURE 16   Percentage of Americans with low serum zinc levels, by sex and age. Data from the second National Health and Nutrition Examination Survey (FASEB, 1984).

Figure 16 shows that the prevalence of low serum zinc values in the NHANES II sample ranged from 1% in males to 4% in females. The prevalence of low values was slightly higher in young children and the elderly than in adolescents and young adults. These observations provide some indication of groups that should be evaluated in greater depth; however, serum zinc levels are only suggestive of poor zinc nutriture for reasons discussed below.

Data on Dietary Intake

No conclusions can be drawn about the adequacy of zinc levels in the American diet because neither NHANES II nor NFCS estimated zinc intakes. At the time those surveys were conducted, the data on the zinc content of foods were not complete enough to make reliable estimates. The only national-level data on zinc are the per capita availability of zinc in the food supply (Welsh and Marston, 1983). Between 1909 and 1981, the zinc level of the food supply fluctuated between 11 and 13 mg per capita per day—a level considerably below the RDA of 15 mg for adults or the RDA of 14.2 mg for the population, which was derived by taking into account the distribution of sex-age groups within the United States in 1981.

Until better methods for measuring nutritional status and more extensive food composition data are available, national surveys will be unable to assess zinc nutritional status.

CONCLUSIONS

For such nutrients as iron, vitamin C, and zinc there are various kinds of survey data, and conclusions about dietary sufficiency can be made with differing levels of confidence. Dietary surveys (e.g., NFCS) indicate groups with low intakes; however, because most persons' nutrient requirements are less than the full RDA, these groups may not, in fact, be malnourished. Thus, dietary surveys only suggest groups at risk for poor nutritional status. In nutritional status surveys (e.g., NHANES II) biochemical tests are used to determine the prevalance of low or impaired nutritional status among groups. Those prevalences are usually much lower than those estimated for at-risk populations in dietary surveys using the RDAs as a basis for low intake. When both kinds of survey data coincide, identifying a group with high prevalence of a biochemical marker of abnormal nutritional status and with low dietary intake, we have strong evidence that a diet-related problem exists. However, we must consider the possibility that some other life-style factor or illness has contributed to the group's low nutritional status.

REFERENCES

FASEB (Federation of American Societies for Experimental Biology). 1984a. Assessment of the Iron Nutritional Status of the U.S. Population Based on Data Collected in the Second National Health and Nutrition Examination Survey, 1976-1980. Life Sciences Research Office. FASEB Special Publications Office, Bethesda, Md.

FASEB (Federation of American Societies for Experimental Biology). 1984b. Assessment of Zinc Nutritional Status of the U.S. Population Based on Data Collected in the Second National Health and Nutrition Examination Survey, 1976-1980. Life Sciences Research Office. FASEB Special Publications Office, Bethesda, Md.

Gallup Organization, Inc. 1982. Gallup Study of Vitamin Use in the U.S. Survey VI, volume 1. Gallup Organization, Inc., Princeton, N.J.

Gunter, E. W., W. E. Turner, J. W. Neese, and D. D. Bayse. 1985. Laboratory Procedures Used by the Clinical Chemistry Division, Centers for Disease Control, for the Second Health and Nutrition Examination Survey (HANES II) 1976-1980. Public Health Service, Centers for Disease Control, Atlanta, Ga.

Johnson, C., C. Woteki, and R. Murphy. 1984. Smoking, vitamin supplement use, and other factors affecting serum vitamin C. Fed. Proc. 43(3):666.

McDowell, A., A. Engel, J. T. Massey, and K. Maurer. 1981. Plan and Operation of the Second National Health and Nutrition Examination Survey, 1976-80. Series 1, No. 15. DHHS Pub.

No. (PHS) 81-1317. Vital and Health Statistics. Public Health Service. U.S. Government Printing Office, Washington, D.C.

NRC (National Research Council). 1980. Recommended Dietary Allowances, 9th ed. A report of the Food and Nutrition Board, Assembly of Life Sciences. National Academy of Sciences, Washington, D.C.

USDA (U.S. Department of Agriculture). 1982. Food Consumption: Households in the United States, Spring 1977. Human Nutrition Information Service, Consumer Nutrition Center, Report No. H-1. U.S. Government Printing Office, Washington, D.C.

USDA (U.S. Department of Agriculture). 1983. Food Intakes: Individuals in 48 States, Year 1977-78. Human Nutrition Information Service, Consumer Nutrition Center, Report No. I-1. U.S. Government Printing Office, Washington, D.C.

Welsh, S. O. 1984. Iron in U.S. diets. Speech to Washington, D.C., Nutrition Group, Washington, D.C., September 26.

Welsh, S. O., and R. M. Marston. 1983. Trends in levels of zinc in the U.S. food supply, 1909-1981. Pp. 15-30 in G. E. Inglett, ed. Nutritional Bioavailability of Zinc. American Chemical Society, Washington, D.C.

II
What Factors Shape Eating Patterns?

Introduction

STANLEY R. JOHNSON

Eating patterns are important indicators of the nutrition status of the U.S. population. Nutrition status is in turn associated with a number of health conditions known to be important determinants of mortality and morbidity in the population, and it influences the capacity of humans to perform and their general physical and psychological well-being. For these reasons, eating patterns and observed changes in eating patterns have broad implications for food and nutrition policy.

The previous section provided background information on the health and nutrition status of the U.S. population from two nationwide surveys. The next section will highlight trends in eating patterns that appear to be occurring. To create a bridge between those two sections, we will now explore factors that may be shaping or causing eating patterns and the observed changes. Increased knowledge of factors that shape eating patterns can contribute to an improved understanding of nutrition status, a more complete capacity for anticipating trends in eating patterns, and finally, better education and intervention programs to improve the nutrition and health status of the U.S. population.

The three presentations that follow are reviews of theories from economics, psychology, and consumer behavior on factors that may be shaping eating patterns. The perspectives provided by these papers should stimulate interest in the study of determinants of eating patterns. Of course, eating patterns can be influenced by the food supply and the changing ways that people acquire food. Eating patterns also may change in response to changes in personal preferences, which are influenced by an array of

43

social, economic, and other conditions. In general, eating patterns are shaped by ways people react to and process information, their interactions with others, and culture. Obviously, isolation of the factors that shape eating patterns of the U.S. population or segments thereof is a highly complex undertaking. It is an important pursuit, however, because a more complete understanding of these factors may lead to improvements in intervention and education programs and to better monitoring of the nutrition and health status of the population.

Themes to recognize in the three presentations are concepts of the individual decision process, the stimuli for these decisions, and the responses generated from reactions to these stimuli. This simple stimulus-response framework is useful for achieving a basic understanding of how each discipline explains individual choice for food consumption in general and in particular. These different approaches have implications for what should be measured in analyses of eating patterns and how this information should be used for analyzing and predicting consumption patterns.

To apply the simple stimulus-response framework, it is useful to understand the approaches used in the three papers that follow. According to the model based on economics, individuals receive benefit or satisfaction from the consumption of food commodities. The basic stimuli in the economic model are prices and income. The observed response is the allocation of the food budget or income to different food items. Extensions of the economic choice theory involve adjustments for factors believed to influence preferences, the technology for processing purchased foods into edible forms, time requirements for food preparation, the education levels of individuals, and investments in food preparation and related equipment. The decision unit for the economic model is the household, the individual, or both.

The presentation dealing with psychology focuses on the basic senses of the individual. Through a number of experiments with humans and laboratory animals, responses to selected stimuli are observed. These responses are related to decisions on whether to consume or not consume particular food items. Extensions of this basic model incorporate factors conditioning the observed responses to these stimuli—from the culture, associations with other individuals, and other features of the decision setting. The essentially trial-and-error approach for infants, and to a more limited extent laboratory animals, is replaced in more complex choice situations by structures and institutions that make trial and error unnecessary. For example, social structures provide information to consumers about whether food items are harmful or good through the licensing of restaurants, labeling of food products, inspection certification of meat products, and other channels.

The consumer behavior approach is one of a number of more pragmatic and eclectic theories. In this decision model, the individual is described as an information processor with a memory and a capacity to generalize on the basis of experience. New information introduced into the system in which the processor functions can alter the objectives of the processor, produce different stimuli, or both, thereby yielding responses in the form of observed choices. This information processor model has been used widely in marketing and advertising food products.

The three choice models are a subset of those developed for understanding human behavior in the social and decision sciences.[1] These sciences are relatively new, and their respective theories are in a seemingly constant state of evolution. It would be tempting to express impatience with these theories and, in fact, the disciplines. However, it must be recognized that the decisions or responses studied are determined by highly complex configurations of stimuli and, most importantly, that the subjects of the study are human and, thus, not subject to the high levels of experimental control applied in physical sciences.

Yet, the approaches represented by these three presentations and others in the behavioral and decision sciences provide many opportunities for research and the development of improved policies designed to improve the health and nutrition status of the population. The three frameworks suggest various measurements and various ways of processing new and older data. In general, they have the potential to improve the scientific basis for public health policy; nutrition education; and intervention programs that are designed to control the food supply, information on the food supply, food assistance programs, and the multitude of factors influencing choices of foods and observed eating patterns.

---

[1]Includes marketing, consumer behavior, public administration, and applications of the social sciences.

Economics and Nutrition

The disciplines of economics and nutrition provide important insights into the understanding of American eating patterns. Major themes that help elucidate these patterns include the effect of income and prices on diet, efficiency in food consumption patterns, and the conceptual perspectives provided by the new household economics and by food and nutrition profiles.

INCOME AND DIET

One of the first factors an economist examines in analyzing food consumption behavior is household income, which determines the budget that is available for expenditures and imposes constraints on consumer behavior. Income may, therefore, be related to nutrient intake and food consumption patterns.

Income and Nutrient Intake

Table 1 presents average nutrient intake levels, as percentages of the Recommended Dietary Allowances (RDAs) (NRC, 1980), for persons in households at four income levels. These data are based on the individual portion of the 1977-1978 Nationwide Food Consumption Survey (NFCS) conducted by the U.S. Department of Agriculture (USDA, 1980) and reflect income levels for that period. Consumption of all nutrients except vitamin A and thiamin appears to increase with income. However, the

TABLE 1 Per Capita Average Daily Nutrient Intake Levels, Measured as Percentages of the 1980 Recommended Dietary Allowances (RDAs), at Four Household Income Levels[a]

	Intake as a Percentage of 1980 RDAs, by Household Income[b]			
Nutrients	Under $6,000	$6,000 to $9,999	$10,000 to $15,999	$16,000 and Over
Food energy	80	84	86	86
Protein	154	163	167	171
Calcium	80	83	89	87
Iron	99	102	105	104
Magnesium	77	79	85	85
Phosphorus	128	132	139	139
Vitamin A	119	115	114	117
Thiamin	115	108	116	111
Riboflavin	125	125	137	130
Niacin	117	122	128	129
Vitamin B_6	70	74	78	79
Vitamin B_{12}	120	132	144	145
Vitamin C	144	140	147	164

[a]From USDA, 1980.
[b]Income data from 1977–1978.

differences with increased income are small and have not been tested for statistical significance; standard deviations were not provided in the NFCS publications. For eight of the nutrients, consumption exceeds the RDAs at all four income levels. By contrast, intakes of calcium, magnesium, and vitamin B_6 are below their RDAs at all four income levels. In general, there is not a strong relationship between nutrient intake and income level.

Some groups of the U.S. population have marked dietary deficiencies—for example, inadequate iron and calcium levels for many women and girls—but these problems are not related to income (USDA, 1980). The United States is sufficiently wealthy so that income level is usually no longer a primary determinant of nutrient intake. However, for those who live in extreme poverty—for example, migrant workers, Indian reservation inhabitants, and homeless city dwellers—severely substandard diets are prevalent (Halcrow, 1977).

The evidence on caloric consumption in Table 1 deserves special comment. The highest level of food energy intake is only 86% of the RDA. This finding does not agree with the generally accepted observation that overconsumption of calories is far more widespread than underconsumption in the United States. A recent food survey indicated that almost two-thirds of those surveyed had tried to lose weight in the past year (Leonard, 1982). Calories are unique among the nutrients, in that persons receive

direct and obvious feedback on their own individual caloric needs through
weight gain or loss.

Income and Food Consumption Patterns

Although there are few substantial differences in nutrient intake by
income level, the same nutrients can be obtained from different foods,
and eating patterns might be markedly different across income groups.
Table 2 presents the dietary intake of major food groups for the same four
income levels as in Table 1. Consumption of beef, cream and milk desserts,
cheese, fats and oils, fruits, soft drinks, and alcoholic beverages increased
more than 25% between the lowest and highest income groups. However,

TABLE 2 Per Capita Average Daily Dietary Intake of Major Food
Groups in Households at Four Income Levels[a]

| Food Group | Average Daily Intake (g) by Household Income Level[b] | | | |
	Under $6,000 (N = 4,026)	$6,000 to $9,999 (N = 4,249)	$10,000 to $15,999 (N = 7,286)	$16,000 and Over (N = 11,624)
Beef	40	46	51	57
Pork	19	20	19	20
Poultry	27	25	24	23
Other meats, fish[c]	96	107	109	112
Milk	254	279	295	291
Cheese	10	13	14	17
Cream and milk desserts	18	19	23	26
Eggs	29	30	24	24
Baked goods	103	112	112	112
Cereals, pastas	70	58	47	42
Fats	10	12	14	15
Vegetables	192	198	196	197
Fruits	122	132	133	158
Legumes, nuts	30	30	26	21
Sugar, sweets	20	23	23	25
Soft drinks	139	166	176	174
Alcoholic beverages	32	33	45	62
Other beverages[d]	360	387	412	436

[a]From USDA, 1983c.
[b]Total annual before-tax money earnings of all members of the household in which the
surveyed person resided. Income data from 1977–1978.
[c]Includes lamb, veal, game, organ meats, organ meat mixtures, frankfurters, sausages,
luncheon meat, fish, shellfish, and mixtures of mainly meat, poultry, and fish. Mixtures
account for highest consumption in this food group.
[d]Includes coffee, tea, fruit drinks, and fruit-ades.

the consumption of poultry, eggs, cereals and pasta, and legumes and nuts tended to decline with increased income.

Income Elasticity. Economists use "income elasticity" (the percentage change in consumption corresponding to a percentage change in income) as a single statistic that reflects the relationship between income and consumption. Table 3 provides income elasticities estimated from the household portion of the 1977-1978 NFCS data (USDA, 1981a). Consumers consider most food groups to be necessities. Economists define a necessity as a good with an income elasticity greater than zero but less than one, so that as income increases consumption also rises, but less rapidly than the increase in income. As shown in Table 3, a few categories—processed milk, cereal products, pork, eggs, and canned fruits and vegetables—are inferior goods with negative elasticities, in which case consumption declines as income increases and vice versa. The highest income elasticities are for alcoholic beverages and food away from home.

TABLE 3 Income Elasticities Estimated from the Household Portion of the 1977–1978 Nationwide Food Consumption Survey[a]

Food Group	Income Elasticity[b]
Total food	0.32
Food away from home	0.81
Food at home	0.15
Dairy products	0.15
Fresh milk	0.05
Processed milk	−0.08
Cheese	0.32
Fats and oils	0.07
Cereal products	−0.12
Bakery products	0.15
Beef	0.23
Pork	−0.01
Poultry	0.07
Fish, shellfish	0.33
Eggs	−0.06
Sugar and sweets	0.05
Fresh vegetables	0.18
Fresh fruits	0.24
Canned fruits and vegetables	−0.04
Frozen fruits and vegetables	0.44
Soft drinks	0.19
Alcoholic beverages	0.90

[a]From USDA, 1981a.
[b]Income elasticity = percentage change in consumption corresponding to a 1% change in income.

Food Consumed Away from Home. The average household purchased and consumed 23% of its total food, measured by dollar cost, away from home in 1977-1978 (USDA, 1983a, p. 13). However, this figure varied dramatically depending on income level. For example, households with annual incomes less than $5,000 purchased and consumed only 12% of their total money value of food away from home, whereas households with incomes of $25,000 and higher spent 31% of their total food dollars on food away from home. When weekly per person costs for food consumed away from home were measured, households with incomes less than $5,000 (13% of all households in the NFCS) spent only $1.93 per person, in contrast to households with incomes of $25,000 and higher (10% of the total survey), which spent $8.94 per person—more than four times as much as the former group (USDA, 1983a, p. 13). The weekly dollar value of food consumed at home was $15.38 per person for the same low-income households and $19.66 per person for the high-income households, a difference of only 28%.

Food Consumed at Home. For some food items consumed at home, there are marked differences in consumption with income level. For example, the NFCS data for 1977-1978 indicated that consumption of fresh skim milk, yogurt, and sirloin steaks increased sharply as income rose (USDA, 1983a). For each of these foods, the difference in consumption between the low and high income levels was threefold or greater (Table 4). In contrast, cornmeal, grits, and sweet potato consumption decreased by at least a factor of three between the lower and higher income levels.

Income is highly correlated with other sociodemographic factors, such as age, education, and race, that are also determinants of food consumption patterns. The patterns observed in Tables 1, 2, and 4 should not be attributed solely, or even predominantly, to income. In Table 4, for ex-

TABLE 4 Per Capita Weekly Consumption of Some Foods at Home at Two Income Levels[a]

Foods	Weekly Consumption (g) by Household Income	
	Under $5,000	$25,000 and Over
Fresh skim milk	82.29	265.14
Yogurt	18.29	54.86
Sirloin steak	22.86	86.86
Cornmeal	86.86	9.14
Grits	27.43	4.57
Sweet potatoes	41.14	13.71

[a]From USDA, 1983a.

ample, it can be seen that cornmeal, grits, and sweet potato consumption is high among rural Southern blacks, a group that contains a disproportionately large portion of the country's poor. Multivariate analysis techniques, such as regression analysis, are necessary to isolate the effect of specific socioeconomic factors on food consumption.

PRICES AND DIET

Food prices, particularly price differences between substitute products, also strongly influence food consumption patterns. Some of the most marked changes in eating patterns during the last 20 years have occurred in meat and poultry consumption. Table 5 presents annual per capita consumption and price data for beef and veal, pork, and poultry. These data were estimated utilizing a food balance sheet or disappearance approach, based on the flow of food items through the food distribution system. Considerable discrepancies may exist between consumption as measured by the balance sheet, household survey, and individual dietary intake methods. The prices in the table are given as consumer price indexes for each product, and 1960 rather than 1967 is equal to a base of 100.

The shifts in consumption of beef and veal, pork, and poultry appear to strongly reflect the relative price changes in the three categories. Between 1960 and 1970 pork prices increased the most and poultry prices increased the least; in the same period, pork consumption barely changed, whereas poultry consumption rose by 44%. Beef price increases were modest and, corresponding to beef's higher income elasticity (Table 3), beef consumption rose 25% between 1960 and 1970 as real income increased.

During the 1970s, pork, with its lower price increases, became a more attractive buy than beef, and poultry became a markedly more attractive

TABLE 5 Meat and Poultry: Annual Per Capita Consumption and Prices, 1960–1982[a]

Foods	Annual Consumption (kg)[b]				Consumer Price Indexes (1960 = 100)[c]			
	1960	1970	1980	1982	1960	1970	1980	1982
Beef and veal	32	39	36	36	100	130	293	300
Pork	27	28	31	27	100	141	255	315
Poultry	16	22	28	29	100	101	178	182

[a]From USDA, 1981b, and USDA, 1983b.
[b]Retail weight.
[c]For ease of comparison, consumer price index figures were recalculated from a 1967 = 100 base to a 1960 = 100 base.

buy than red meats, especially beef. Partially in reaction to these price changes, beef consumption between 1970 and 1980 declined 9%, pork increased 10%, and poultry increased 25%. Between 1980 and 1982, the sharp price jump in pork induced a marked drop in consumption.

Unquestionably, other factors have affected these consumption shifts. However, a recent USDA study argued that "an overwhelming part of the variation in U.S. meat demand can be explained by changes in retail prices and consumer incomes" (Haidacher *et al.*, 1982, p. iv).

EFFICIENCY IN FOOD CONSUMPTION

This section explores various perspectives on the efficiency of food consumption patterns in terms of the observed pattern of nutrients per dollar's worth of food, the USDA food plans, and least-cost diets.

Dietary Efficiency

Table 6 indicates the efficiency with which households at different income levels use their food budgets to obtain basic nutrients. The general pattern that emerges is that lower income households spend their food budgets more efficiently than higher income households by obtaining more nutrients per dollar's worth of food. The milligrams of thiamin per dollar of food, for example, declined from 0.89 to 0.72 mg between the lowest and highest income groups. The efficiency increase of lower income households is probably even greater than suggested by Table 6, which only reflects food used at home. As discussed previously, higher income households consume more of their meals away from home. And food consumed away from home, on the average, is substantially more expensive on a nutrient per dollar basis than food consumed at home.

The USDA Food Plans

The USDA (Cleveland and Peterkin, 1983) publishes four food plans—thrifty, low-cost, moderate-cost, and liberal—which provide nutritious diets at four cost levels. The food plans were developed using data on the observed food consumption patterns at various income levels. Recently revised plans were based on the 1977-1978 NFCS (USDA, 1983a,c). The food plans are designed to satisfy dietary standards (according to the RDAs for the major nutrients) at a given cost with the fewest possible changes from observed consumption patterns (Cleveland and Peterkin, 1983).

Compared to actual consumption patterns, the food plans contain fewer

TABLE 6 Dietary Efficiency: Nutrients Per Dollar's Worth of Food Consumed at Home for Households at Five Income Levels, Spring 1977[a]

Household Income	Food Energy (kcal)	Protein (g)	Calcium (mg)	Iron (mg)	Magnesium (mg)	Phosphorus (mg)	Vitamin A Value (IU)	Thiamin (mg)	Riboflavin (mg)	Niacin (mg)	Vitamin B$_6$ (mg)	Vitamin B$_{12}$ (mg)	Ascorbic Acid (mg)
Under $5,000	1,280	45	470	9.1	170	780	3,720	0.89	1.16	12	0.97	3.0	61
$5,000–$9,999	1,310	45	460	9.1	180	770	3,630	0.86	1.14	12	0.98	2.8	62
$10,000–$14,999	1,300	45	480	9.1	180	780	3,200	0.86	1.14	12	0.96	2.7	59
$15,000–$19,999	1,220	42	450	8.1	160	730	2,860	0.75	1.06	11	0.89	2.5	55
$20,000 or more	1,140	41	440	7.7	160	700	2,930	0.72	1.03	11	0.87	2.4	56

[a]From USDA, 1979, p. 12.

soft drinks, sugar and sweets, fats and oils, cheese, eggs, and meat, but more grain products and dry beans, peas, and nuts. These changes tend to lower costs and improve the nutritional content of the diet. In addition, these dietary changes would bring food consumption patterns more in line with the *Dietary Goals for the United States* developed by the Senate Select Committee on Nutrition and Human Needs (U.S. Congress, 1977). These dietary goals, subsequently referred to as dietary guidelines, advocated an increase in complex carbohydrate consumption (primarily from grain products) and a reduction in the consumption of sugar, fat (particularly saturated fat), cholesterol, and salt.

Least-Cost Diets

An approach different from that of the USDA food plans has been the construction of least-cost or very low cost diet plans using linear programming techniques (Foytik, 1981). The objective function in the program is to minimize the cost of the diet, subject to the constraint of satisfying basic nutritional requirements with the given food prices. The solution is not restricted to correspond with observed eating patterns. Additional constraints that are typically added impose upper and lower quantity limits on particular foods to ensure a more varied and palatable diet.

A recently developed very low cost diet plan met the same nutrient standards as the thrifty food plan at only 60% of its cost (Foytik, 1981). Adoption of such a diet, however, would require a substantial change in food consumption for even low-income households. For example, the diet allows powdered milk as the only dairy product and excludes meat other than chicken, hamburger, and beef chuck.

The USDA food plans (Cleveland and Peterkin, 1983) recognize that cultural, psychological, and social factors affect food choices and that food consumption patterns are deeply ingrained and difficult to change. The typical household is limited in its ability and desire to pursue a more efficient diet. Significantly, the U.S. Food Stamp Program allotments are based on the USDA thrifty food plan; no one has seriously proposed that a least-cost diet be the basis for the program allotments.

IMPORTANT CONCEPTUAL PERSPECTIVES

A brief overview of two conceptual perspectives, the new household economics and food and nutrition profiles, provides further insight into American eating patterns.

The New Household Economics

Gary Becker's model of time allocation, one of the more important additions to economic theory in the past 25 years, has given rise to the new household economics (Becker, 1965; Michael and Becker, 1973). This model has important implications for understanding eating patterns. The household is viewed as a production, as well as a consumption, entity that combines market-purchased goods and household time to produce the actual consumables. In the model, time is as crucial a constraint on consumption behavior as is the budget. When time is scarce, it becomes more valuable, and a shift toward a less time-intensive consumption pattern occurs.

The purchase and preparation of food for consumption at home requires a substantial input of household time. One can view food choices as reflecting a fairly continuous range of required household production times. At the most time-intensive extreme, for example, are homegrown products, followed by meals prepared from scratch—such as baking bread at home—and then home cooking, which entails the use of some prepared foods, such as store-bought bread and canned or frozen vegetables. At the time-saving end of the range are convenience foods, such as prepared frozen dinners, followed by the least time-intensive extreme—food consumed away from home.

Prochaska and Schrimper (1973) found that as the value of a woman's time rose, as measured by her wage rate or potential wage, the household purchased more meals away from home. One of the major trends today is the increased participation of women, particularly married women, in the work force. The resulting increased scarcity of household time partially explains the steadily increasing proportion of food eaten away from home and the current high demand for such products as microwave ovens and frozen dinner entrees.

Food and Nutrition Profiles

Some recent research by the Community Nutrition Institute (Leonard, 1982) indicated that American households follow particular, distinctive eating patterns. Households were divided into five food and nutrition profiles based on their dietary practices. "Meat eaters" (30% of surveyed households) were heavy consumers of meat, sugar, and sweets. "People on the go" (14% of the sample) ate more meals away from home and spent more for food than other groups. "In a dither" households (16% of the sample) had a high convenience-food consumption. The "conscientious" (15% of the sample) spent less for food, had more nutrition knowledge, ate more at home, and cooked and baked more. "Healthy eaters" (25% of the sample) ate less meat, fat, sugar, and sweets, but ate more vegetables, fruits, and whole grains than did other households.

The socioeconomic characteristics appear to be quite consistent for the households that fall into each of these food and nutrition profiles. For example, healthy eaters are typically from small households with older members. The conscientious include more high income families. In-a-dither households typically have many members, whereas on-the-go households have fewer members.

CONCLUSIONS

Historically, and in many societies of the world today, human food consumption consists of a simple diet usually dominated by a single staple, such as rice, wheat, or corn. Only the rich in such societies can afford more varied diets. In sharp contrast, contemporary American eating patterns reflect the remarkably varied diets that occur when economic abundance is widespread, although certainly not universal, in a society. Eating patterns in the United States demonstrate the complexity of human behavior and continue to challenge researchers' understanding and explanation of them. Given the generally plentiful American food supply, public concern should focus particularly on the diets and nutritional needs of the poor, who do not share in this abundance.

REFERENCES

Becker, G. 1965. A theory of the allocation of time. Econ. J. 74:493-517.

Cleveland, L. E., and B. Peterkin. 1983. USDA 1983 family food plans. U.S. Department of Agriculture, Agricultural Research Service. Fam. Econ. Rev. 2:12-21.

Foytik, J. 1981. Very low-cost nutritious diet plans designed by linear programming. J. Nutr. Educ. 13:63-65.

Haidacher, R. C., J. A. Craven, K. S. Huang, D. M. Smallwood, and J. R. Blaylock. 1982. Consumer Demand for Red Meats, Poultry, and Fish. Economic Research Service, National Economics Division. U.S. Department of Agriculture, Washington, D.C.

Halcrow, H. G. 1977. Food Policy. McGraw-Hill, New York.

Leonard, R. 1982. Nutrition profiles: Diet in the 80s. Community Nutritionist 1:12-17.

Michael, R., and G. Becker. 1973. On the new theory of consumer behavior. Swed. J. Econ. 75:378-396.

NRC (National Research Council). 1980. Recommended Dietary Allowances, 9th ed. A report of the Food and Nutrition Board, Assembly of Life Sciences. National Academy of Sciences, Washington, D.C.

Prochaska, F. J., and R. A. Schrimper. 1973. Opportunity cost of time and other socioeconomic effects on away-from-home food consumption. Am. J. Agric. Econ. 55:595-603.

U.S. Congress. 1977. Dietary Goals for the United States. Senate Select Committee on Nutrition and Human Needs, 95th Congress, 1st Session.

USDA (U.S. Department of Agriculture). 1979. Money Value of Food Used by Households in the United States, Spring 1977. Science and Education Administration, Nationwide Food Consumption Survey 1977-78, Preliminary Report No. 1. U.S. Department of Agriculture, Hyattsville, Md.

USDA (U.S. Department of Agriculture). 1980. Food and Nutrient Intake of Individuals in One Day in the United States, Spring 1977. Science and Education Administration, Nationwide Food Consumption Survey 1977-78, Preliminary Report No. 2. U.S. Department of Agriculture, Hyattsville, Md.

USDA (U.S. Department of Agriculture). 1981a. Impact of Household Size and Income on Food Spending Patterns. Economics and Statistics Service, Technical Bulletin No. 1650. U.S. Department of Agriculture, Washington, D.C.

USDA (U.S. Department of Agriculture). 1981b. Food Consumption, Prices, and Expenditures, 1960-1980. Economic Research Service, Statistical Bulletin No. 672. U.S. Department of Agriculture, Washington, D.C.

USDA (U.S. Department of Agriculture). 1983a. Food Consumption: Households in the United States, Seasons and Year 1977-78. Human Nutrition Information Service, Consumer Nutrition Division, Nationwide Food Consumption Survey 1977-78, Report No. H-6. U.S. Department of Agriculture, Hyattsville, Md.

USDA (U.S. Department of Agriculture). 1983b. Food Consumption, Prices, and Expenditures, 1962-1982. Economic Research Service, Statistical Bulletin No. 702. U.S. Department of Agriculture, Washington, D.C.

USDA (U.S. Department of Agriculture). 1983c. Food Intakes: Individuals in 48 States, Year 1977-78. Human Nutrition Information Service, Consumer Nutrition Division, Nationwide Food Consumption Survey 1977-78, Report No. I-1. U.S. Department of Agriculture, Hyattsville, Md.

The Acquisition of Likes
and Dislikes for Foods

PAUL ROZIN and APRIL FALLON

In the act of eating, substances from the outside world enter the body through the mouth. For all practical purposes, the last opportunity for food selection is presented when these substances reach the mouth; it is difficult to reject them once they have passed through the mouth. Since the substances that enter the mouth may contain essential nutrients, toxins, or harmful microorganisms, it is not surprising that the acts of tasting, eating, and swallowing are laden with emotion. This is particularly true for humans, who, as omnivores, ingest a wide variety of substances. Humans and other food generalists must discover which of the various substances in the environment are beneficial or harmful. There is no way of coding most of this information in the genes; there are just too many different kinds of edible and inedible substances. Rather, food generalists rely on their abilities to evaluate substances in terms of their postingestional consequences. It is a basic feature of these species, including humans, that they have minimal genetic determination of food recognition.

At birth, the human infant has a few genetically programmed biases, such as a positive response to sweet tastes and a negative response to bitter, irritant, and perhaps other very strong tastes (e.g., Cowart, 1981). With the exception of these few innate rejections, children in our culture up to approximately 2 years of age seem to regard everything as potentially edible. Therefore, a major challenge of early development is learning what not to eat (Rozin *et al.*, in press). Maturation, individual experience, and cultural and familial influences build on a minimal biological base so that by early adulthood, humans in every culture have acquired a culturally based set of beliefs and attitudes that enable them to categorize substances with respect to edibility.

PSYCHOLOGICAL CATEGORIES OF ACCEPTED AND REJECTED FOOD SUBSTANCES

Through interviews and questionnaires, we explored the psychological categorization of substances as foods and nonfoods in American culture (Fallon and Rozin, 1983; Rozin and Fallon, 1980, 1981). Three basic types of reasons for acceptance or rejection of objects emerged: (1) sensory properties of a substance; (2) anticipated consequences of ingestion; and (3) ideas about the nature or origin of the substance. Each of these reasons in one form motivates acceptance and in the opposite form motivates rejection (Table 1). This simplified system emphasizes the principal feature motivating acceptance or rejection. Certainly, many choices are determined by more than one of these factors, as when one accepts milk because it both tastes good (a sensory property) and promotes health (anticipated consequences).

Sensory Properties

Some items are rejected or accepted primarily because of their sensory effects in the mouth or because of their odor or appearance. Accepted items are "good tastes" and rejected items are "distastes" (Table 1). (We use the word tastes loosely here to include all mouth sensations, including the odor of the food in the mouth.) Good tastes and distastes, by definition, produce appropriate positive and negative feelings (like or dislike). These feelings can be acquired or innately associated with certain objects (e.g., acceptance of sweet tastes, rejection of bitter); others are acquired. Substances that a person likes or dislikes on the basis of their sensory effects are almost always acceptable foods in the person's culture. Differences in preference for these substances among members of the same culture probably account for most variations in food preference within a culture (e.g., liking or disliking lima beans).

Anticipated Consequences

Some substances are accepted or rejected as food primarily because of anticipated consequences of ingestion. These could be the pleasant feeling of satiation or rapid-onset unpleasant effects, such as nausea, cramps, and allergic responses (e.g., rashes). The consequences could also be delayed effects, involving beliefs and attitudes about the health value of substances

TABLE 1 Psychological Categorization of Rejected and Accepted Substances[a]

Motivation for Acceptance or Rejection	Categories of Rejection				Categories of Acceptance			
	Distaste	Danger	Inappropriate	Disgust	Good Taste	Beneficial	Appropriate	Transvalued
Sensory properties	+			+	+			+
Anticipated consequences		+				+		
Ideational		?[b]	+	+		?[b]	+	+
	Examples:	Examples:	Examples:	Examples:	Examples:	Examples:	Examples:	Examples:
	Beer, chili, quinine water	Allergy foods, carcinogens	Grass, sand	Feces, insects	Saccharin	Medicines	Ritual foods	Leavings of heroes or deities

[a]Adapted from Rozin and Fallon, 1981, and Fallon and Rozin, 1983.
[b]May be involved in response.

(such as vitamins or low-fat foods on the positive side or potential carcinogens on the negative side). In some cases, culturally transmitted knowledge about a food (e.g., that it is carcinogenic) accounts for rejection, in which case there is an ideational component to the rejection (see Table 1). Anticipated consequences need not be physiological; they may be social, such as expected changes in social status as a consequence of eating or not eating a food. In Table 1, substances that are accepted on the basis of their anticipated consequences are in the beneficial category, whereas those that are rejected for similar reasons are listed in the danger category. There may or may not be a liking for the taste of these items.

Ideational Factors

Some substances are rejected or accepted primarily because of our knowledge of the nature or source of the item. Ideational factors predominate in many food rejections but are rarely central in acceptance. Categories of foods accepted because of knowledge concerning their nature or origin are what we call appropriate and transvalued. These are discussed in the last section of this chapter.

We distinguished two subcategories of ideational rejections: those based on the inappropriateness of an item and those that elicit disgust. Inappropriate items are considered inedible within a culture and are refused simply on this basis. Grass and sand are examples. There is no presumption that these items taste bad, and a person usually regards them as neutral and inoffensive. In contrast, substances in the subcategory of disgust evoke a strong negative emotional response, are offensive, and are thought to have unpleasant tastes, although in most instances they have never been tasted. Feces, insects, worms, and meat from reptiles and dogs are examples found in American culture. (A third type of ideational rejection, not mentioned in Table 1, is based on respect; a species of animal is rejected as food because it is a totem or has some special sacred properties.)

DEVELOPMENT OF ADULT PREFERENCES AND ATTITUDES TOWARD FOOD

The infant's simple acceptance or rejection of substances on the basis of their taste (sensory) properties develops into the rather elaborate adult system of preferences and attitudes toward foods. In this chapter, we consider what is known about the circumstances in which objects come to have good or bad tastes, in contrast to those in which they are accepted or rejected on the basis of anticipated consequences or ideational factors. Three contrasting pairs of categories are examined: distaste and danger;

good taste and beneficial; and disgust and inappropriate. In each case, the first of the pair involves an emotional response (taste like or dislike), but the second of the pair does not.

Distaste Versus Danger

Many initially acceptable items are later rejected—some because they are recategorized from good to bad tastes, others because a person learns that they are dangerous. What determines whether an object will acquire one or both of these properties?

Humans, rats, and many other omnivores learn rapidly to avoid foods that make them sick. One episode of becoming ill minutes to hours after ingesting a new food is sufficient in most cases to motivate avoidance (Garcia *et al.*, 1974; Rozin and Kalat, 1971). We explored more than 200 instances of acquired rejections of food reported in questionnaires by people who had associated certain foods with unpleasant events such as food poisoning, food allergies, appearance of the symptoms of an infectious disease (e.g., the flu) shortly after eating, and falling down or having an accident while eating (Pelchat and Rozin, 1982; Rozin and Fallon, 1980). If nausea or vomiting followed consumption of a food, a person would usually come to dislike its taste, but if other negative events occurred (e.g., gut cramps, headache, hives, difficulty breathing) in the absence of nausea, a person tended to avoid the food, but not dislike its taste.

This contrast can be illustrated by typical cases of two people who avoid apples. One has an allergy to apples and develops a skin rash or respiratory distress after eating them. Such a person will avoid apples as dangerous while liking their taste. If the allergy could be treated, this person would be delighted to consume apples. The other person originally liked apples, but became sick and vomited after eating them. This person will typically dislike the taste of apples and avoid them, although realizing that they are in fact not dangerous and were perhaps not even the cause of the sickness.

Although these findings suggest that nausea is a critical factor in determining whether a food will become distasteful, it is unlikely that most acquired distastes were once associated with nausea. Fewer than half of the questionnaire respondents could remember even one instance of a food avoidance based on nausea, and these same people had many distastes. Presumably, then, many persons who dislike foods like lima beans, fish, and broccoli are doing so for reasons as yet undiscovered.

Although adults often consider the same food as both distasteful and dangerous, in many instances they distinguish these two categories. For children younger than 8 years, however, there is a tendency to confound the categories; such children often believe that if a food is bad for them, it will also taste bad (Fallon *et al.*, 1984).

Good Taste Versus Beneficial

There is no single cause of acquired good tastes that has the salience or potency that nausea has as a cause for acquired distastes. The overriding empirical relation in the study of acquired likes is that exposure tends to increase liking. Zajonc (1968) in his "mere exposure" theory has suggested that exposure is a *sufficient* condition for liking. Enhanced liking of foods resulting from exposure has been demonstrated in the laboratory for both children (Birch and Marlin, 1982) and adults (Pliner, 1982). However, overexposure can result in a diminution of liking (e.g., Stang, 1975). It is also not clear whether "mere exposure" is sufficient or whether it allows another process to occur (such as those mentioned below).

There is evidence that other specific factors could increase liking. A critical variable might be the "opposite" of nausea, such as the pleasant feeling of fullness and satiation after eating. Booth and his colleagues (Booth, 1982; Booth *et al.*, 1982) have demonstrated that rapid satiety enhances preference and liking in rats and humans. A study on the acquisition of liking for flavors of a variety of medicines provided no evidence that any other postingestional effects (e.g., fever reduction, reduction in heartburn) enhance the liking for flavors (Pliner *et al.*, in press). Although satiety seems to be specifically linked with the generation of good tastes, its effect is much less striking than the effect of nausea on distastes.

There are certainly other causes of acquired good tastes. For example, a neutral food or flavor can become liked if it is associated with an already liked food or flavor through the process of Pavlovian conditioning. This has been demonstrated by Zellner *et al.* (1983), whose subjects tasted flavor A in a sweet, palatable beverage and flavor B in an unsweetened, less palatable beverage. In subsequent tests, the same subjects liked flavor A more than flavor B, even when both flavors were served in the unsweetened form.

One problem with assigning a primary role for satiety, other postingestional effects, or flavor-flavor associations in the acquisition of liking for foods is that it has been very difficult to establish strong acquired preferences in animals, in contrast to the ease in production of avoidances (Rozin *et al.*, 1979; Zahorik, 1979; but see Booth, 1982). If physiological effects or positive flavor associations were indeed the main determinant of liking, one would expect animals to exhibit the phenomenon as well as humans. Again, there are almost certainly other causes of acquiring good tastes.

Given the high frequency of acquired likes in humans, but not in other animals, we are inclined to assign an important role to social and cultural factors. Cultural forces exert a powerful control on the availability of food and hence on exposure. Insofar as exposure *per se* leads to preference, this alone would be a substantial effect of culture. In addition, the social forces that in general account for the transmission of cultural values presumably operate in the domain of food. Thus, for example, social pressure may initially induce a child to consume a socially approved food; later other social forces may induce an acquired like (good taste), so that social pressure is no longer necessary to maintain ingestion. This sequence clearly describes what occurs in our culture with the individual's acceptance of cigarettes.

Some evidence suggests that the apparent liking of a food by respected people (e.g., parents, older peers) is a critical sociocultural factor. Preschool children tend to increase their preference for a particular snack if the teacher uses the snack itself as a reward, thereby indicating that the teacher has a high opinion of the object (Birch *et al.*, 1980). Mere exposure in a nonsocial setting (e.g., when the food item is placed in the child's locker every day) did not produce an increased liking.

Other evidence for the importance of the perceived social value of a food comes from research on decreases in liking for food. How can an object of intrinsic value (which we call a liked object) lose some of this value? One answer is that if children believe that they eat something for extrinsic reasons (such as achieving a desired reward), this belief tends to destroy the intrinsic (liked) value of the food (Lepper, 1980). When preschool children were rewarded for eating a particular food, preference for that food increased while the reward was in effect but dropped below initial levels after the reward was removed (Birch *et al.*, 1982). Such findings suggest that liking will be increased if children believe that they are eating something for its own sake but will be decreased if the eating appears to be governed by some extrinsic factor.

Any satisfactory explanation of the acquisition of likes must account for various innately aversive substances, such as alcohol, tobacco, coffee, and the irritant spices that are among the more popular foods of humans around the world (Rozin, 1978). Rozin and Schiller (1980) investigated how people come to like the initially distasteful burn of chili pepper. This occurs by age 5 to 8 years in many chili-eating cultures. Capsaicin, the active agent in chili pepper, stimulates the gastrointestinal system, causing salivation, increased gastric secretion, and gut motility. The salivation enhances the flavor of the frequently bland and mealy diets that are usually eaten with chili pepper. This enhancement, together with the taste of the pepper and the satiation produced by the food, may contribute to liking.

Social factors, however, may be more important in the acquisition of liking for chili pepper. A study in a Mexican village suggests that chili eating is not explicitly rewarded, but is acquired in a social context where respected adults and older children eat and enjoy it (Rozin and Schiller, 1980).

Ironically, the initial negativity of chili pepper and other innately unpalatable substances may be a critical element in the process of acquiring a liking for them. The initial mouth pain produced by the chili may become pleasant as the person realizes that it is not really harmful. The pleasure of eating chili pepper then could be regarded as a kind of thrill seeking, like roller coaster riding or recreational parachute jumping. Some people may come to enjoy experiences when their bodies are signalling danger but their minds know there is really no danger (Rozin and Schiller, 1980).

Alternatively, the many painful mouth experiences produced by chili peppers may cause the brain to attempt to modulate the pain by secreting endogenous opiates—morphine-like substances produced in the brain. There is evidence that, like morphine, these brain opiates reduce pain and at high levels might produce pleasure. Hundreds of experiences of chili-based mouth pain may cause stronger and stronger brain opiate responses, resulting in a net pleasure response after many experiences (Rozin et al., 1982; see Solomon, 1980, for a statement of opponent process theory, which could account for the hypothesized effect).

An understanding of the development of liking for foods is far from complete. There are convincing arguments against all the mechanisms we have suggested. Our experience in trying to understand the liking for chili pepper convinces us that there are multiple routes to liking.

Disgust Versus Inappropriate

All previous categories discussed probably apply to animals as well as to humans. The categories of disgust and inappropriate, however, are ideationally based and require the mediation of culture. The critical difference between these categories is that disgusting items are offensive, whereas inappropriate items are essentially neutral. This offensiveness includes the idea of the disgusting substance in the body and its sensory properties: taste, smell, and appearance. The thought of consuming disgusting, but not inappropriate, substances typically leads to nausea. Objects of disgust are contaminants; that is, a physical trace of a disgusting item can render an otherwise liked food undesirable. This physical trace contamination corresponds to what has been referred to by Frazer (1922) and Mauss (1972) as one of the two laws of sympathetic magic: the law of contagion. Frazer summarizes this as ''once in contact, always in contact.'' Furthermore, an acceptable food shaped to look like a disgusting substance (e.g., fudge shaped to look like a cockroach) is often offensive (Rozin and Fallon, 1985). Here similarity elicits disgust, illustrating the second law of sympathetic magic: the law of similarity. This law is succinctly described by Mauss (1972) in his statement, ''The image is equal to the object'' (Rozin and Fallon, 1985).

The disgust and inappropriate categories contain different kinds of items. Objects of disgust (which are often, in many cultures, tabooed substances) are almost always of animal origin (Angyal, 1941; Rozin and Fallon, 1980). Inappropriate items, by contrast, are usually vegetable or inorganic in nature. Using criteria for disgust such as contamination and nausea, Rozin and Fallon (1980) found that pork had disgust properties for many kosher Jews as did meat for some vegetarians.

Origin of Disgust.   Angyal (1941) suggested that disgust is fundamentally a ''fear of oral incorporation of an offensive substance.'' This is in keeping with the facial disgust response, which seems designed to keep offensive substances from the mouth. In general, the more intimate the contact with a disgust substance, and hence the more real the threat of incorporation, the greater the disgust (Fallon and Rozin, 1983). It is likely that the fear is based on the primitive belief, ''You are what you eat.'' Hence, consumption of an offensive substance would make the eater offensive.

We do not have a satisfactory explanation of the origin of disgust. A major feature of such an explanation should be an economical description of the general nature of the objects of disgust, presumably more specific than animals and animal products (reviewed in Rozin and Fallon, 1981, 1985).

One view is that disgust originates as an innate aversion to spoiled, decaying matter. However, nonhumans do not systematically avoid decaying substances. Furthermore, there is evidence indicating that young children are either attracted to feces and decay odors or have neutral responses to them (Petó, 1936; Senn and Solnit, 1968).

Our view is that feces are the primary disgust substance and that the aversion is acquired during the emotion-laden toilet training experience. Adult humans' universal disgust for feces argues in favor of this view (Angyal, 1941). During toilet training, the initial attraction to feces may be changed into a strong aversion (disgust)—a paradigmatic instance of what Freud described as a reaction formation (see Ferenczi, 1952; Senn and Solnit, 1968). A generalization of disgust to other objects perceptually and conceptually similar to feces may occur.

A third view emphasizes filth and disorder as opposed to the narrower concept of decay. Association with filth (e.g., garbage, feces) would be a means of extending the category. Douglas (1966) explicitly identified "filth" as disorder, anomaly, or matter out of place, taking a more conceptual-symbolic approach to this idea.

A fourth view focuses on "animalness" (Angyal, 1941; Rozin and Fallon, 1985). Angyal noted that as the "animalness" is removed from the offensive object, such as by cooking or chopping, the object becomes less disgusting. For example, baked fish is more likely to elicit a disgust response if it is served intact on a platter than if the bones, scales, and head are removed.

In a fifth view, disgust is viewed as an emotionally laden aspect of human social relations. Thus, many objects of disgust are human products or involve human mediation of one sort or another. Food is clearly a major means of social expression. For example, in India (Appadurai, 1981; Khare, 1976) or in New Guinea (Meigs, 1978), consumption of a food produced, touched, or handled by a specific person other than the consumer can entail some notion of incorporating this other being into oneself. Thus, the value of the food depends on the nature of the relation to that other person (Appadurai, 1981; Meigs, 1978). If produced or handled by someone hostile, the food can have dangerous and sometimes disgusting properties.

Possibly each of the five views described above contains part of the truth. All, except the innate spoilage view, entail some sort of acquisition or enculturation process. It seems likely that verbal and nonverbal signals from parents and others, especially negative facial expressions (disgust faces), play a role in communicating disgust to children. By age 4, children reject substances disgusting to adults, although their reasons for doing so may not be the same as those of adults (Fallon *et al.*, 1984). They fail to respond to these substances as contaminants.

We have not explained the mystery of how certain cognitions tap into the strong negative emotional system that we call disgust. We know that when they do, a strong aversion results. This aversion tends to be permanent and to resist modification by rational means. It is ironic that disgust presupposes a rather sophisticated cognitive base—an ability to categorize the world—and yet is so resistant to further cognitive influence.

Transvaluation, the Opposite of Disgust, and the Positive-Negative Balance

As noted in the section on distaste versus danger, animals exhibit a strong bias toward more rapid and more substantial learning about the negative properties of foods than about the positive aspects. In rats, an innate positive response to sweet tastes can be changed to a strong aversion in one learning trial, but an innate aversion (e.g., bitter or irritant tastes) is very difficult to reverse. When there is success, the effect is small and the training extensive (e.g., Rozin *et al.*, 1979; Zahorik, 1979). Presumably, this bias is related to the adaptive value of rapid learning about harmful properties of potential edibles.

Do humans have the same bias? As we have pointed out, humans do learn to reverse innate dislikes. Not only do they come to like or even love many foods, but they develop strong likings for many types of objects (e.g., pets, people, sports teams, music). Thus, in many ways we seem to have overcome the negative bias. But have we? We still learn aversions much more rapidly than preferences. And although there are a large number of items in the world that we reject as offensive (disgusting), and that can contaminate good food, there are practically no instances in American culture of the opposite of disgust. That is, there are few if any substances that in trace amounts make a disliked food likeable. As succinctly put by a garage mechanic in Nebraska, "A teaspoon of sewage would spoil a barrel of wine, but a teaspoon of wine would do nothing at all for a barrel of sewage."

However, even within American culture one can perceive weak signs of positive transvaluation. Thus, some body substances of lovers take on positive, rather than disgust properties. We occasionally feel that a food is better because "grandma made it." Positive transvaluation of food does occur in a more salient way in other cultures, as in the enhancement of the value of food given as a ritual offering in a Hindu temple (Breckenridge, 1978). The clearest example comes from the work of Meigs (1978, 1984) on the Hua of New Guinea. For these people, the vital essence of a person, or *nu*, extends into all the things with which they interact. Hence, the food one has grown, killed, or cooked contains some of one's vital essence. Food that contains the *nu* of those in a positive relation to the eater can nourish, whereas food that contains the *nu* of persons in a potentially hostile relation to the eater can harm. Here we have, in a potent and salient way, something like positive contamination. However, even among the Hua, the negative effects are more potent than the positive. Among the Hua, it is not the object *per se* that is disgusting (or positively transvalued) but its historical context (Meigs, 1978, 1984).

Regardless of the status of positively transvalued food, the weakening of the negative bias in humans is clear. The gained strength of the positive system in humans may be related to culture (Rozin, 1982). Enculturation amounts to the learning of many rules, at least some of which become internalized as positive and negative values. What better way to ensure enculturation than to have the culture's members want (like) what the culture values and dislike what it rejects. Such internalization obviates the necessity for rules and proscriptions to ensure compliance. Perhaps there is a relationship between the presence of culture and the abundance of acquired likes in humans.

SUMMARY

Acceptance or rejection of potential foods by humans can be motivated by sensory properties (like or dislike of the taste and smell), anticipated consequences of ingestion, and culturally transmitted (ideationally based) information about the nature or origin of a particular substance. We consider how substances come to be accepted or rejected and, in particular, what determines whether a person acquires a like or dislike (sensory-hedonic motivation) for a food. Nausea following experience of a flavor is a particularly potent cause of an acquired dislike for that flavor. There is no factor nearly as potent as nausea to account for how some flavors come to be liked; but rapid satiety, association with already liked flavors, and a variety of sociocultural factors have been implicated. Ideational rejections are subcategorized into inappropriate (inedible, usually non-animal, and not offensive) items and disgust (often nutritive, usually animal, and offensive) items. Disgusting items have the contamination property—if they contact an acceptable food it becomes unacceptable. In general, dislikes for foods are acquired much more rapidly than likes, and ideationally based rejections of food (disgust) are more frequent and compelling than corresponding acceptances. This greater potency of negative events is even more marked in animals. Humans may be unique in having a large number of strong likes, including some substances that are innately aversive.

REFERENCES

Angyal, A. 1941. Disgust and related aversions. J. Abnorm. Soc. Psychol. 36:393-412.

Appadurai, A. 1981. Gastropolitics in Hindu South Asia. Am. Ethnol. 8:494-511.

Birch, L. L., and D. W. Marlin. 1982. I don't like it; I never tried it: The effects of familiarity on two-year-old's food preference. Appetite 3:353-360.

Birch, L. L., S. I. Zimmerman, and H. Hind. 1980. The influence of social-affective context on the formation of children's food preferences. Child Dev. 51:856-861.

Birch, L. L., D. Birch, D. W. Marlin, and L. Kramer. 1982. Effects of instrumental consumption on children's food preference. Appetite 3:125-134.

Booth, D. A. 1982. Normal control of omnivore intake by taste and smell. Pp. 233-243 in J. Steiner and J. Ganchrow, eds. The determination of behavior by chemical stimuli. ECRO Symposium. Information Retrieval, London.

Booth, D. A., P. Mather, and J. Fuller. 1982. Starch content of ordinary foods associatively conditions humans' appetite and satiation, indexed by intake and eating pleasantness of starch-paired flavors. Appetite 3:163-184.

Breckenridge, C. A. 1978. Food handling in a Hindu temple: An analysis of sacred cuisine, 1350-1650 A.D. Paper presented at the meeting of the 10th International Conference on Anthropological and Ethnological Sciences, New Delhi, India.

Cowart, B. J. 1981. Development of taste perception in humans. Sensitivity and preference throughout the life span. Psychol. Bull. 90:43-73.

Douglas, M. 1966. Purity and Danger. Routledge and Keegan Paul, London.

Fallon, A. E., and P. Rozin. 1983. The psychological bases of food rejections by humans. Ecol. Food Nutr. 13:15-26.

Fallon, A. E., P. Rozin, and P. Pliner. 1984. The child's conception of food: The development of food rejections with special reference to disgust and contamination sensitivity. Child Devel. 55:566-575.

Ferenczi, S. 1952. The ontogenesis of the interest in money. Pp. 319-331 in S. Ferenczi, ed., E. Jones, trans. First Contributions of Psychoanalysis. Hogarth, London. (Reprinted from Artzl, Z. F. 1914. Psychoanalyse.)

Frazer, J. G. 1922. The Golden Bough: A Study in Magic and Religion. Macmillan, New York.

Garcia, J., W. G. Hankins, and K. W. Rusiniak. 1974. Behavioral regulation of the milieu interne in man and rat. Science 185:824-831.

Khare, R. S. 1976. The Hindu Hearth and Home. Carolina Academic Press, Durham, N.C.

Lepper, M. R. 1980. Intrinsic and extrinsic motivation in children: Detrimental effects of superfluous social controls. Pp. 155-214 in W. A. Collins, ed. Minnesota Symposium on Child Psychology, Vol. 14. Erlbaum, Hillsdale, N.J.

Mauss, M. 1972. A General Theory of Magic. R. Brain, trans. W. W. Norton, New York. (Original work published 1902.) Translation of Equisse d'une Théorie Générale de la Magie, published in L'Année Sociologique, 1902-1903.

Meigs, A. S. 1978. A Papuan perspective on pollution. Man 13:304-318.

Meigs, A. S. 1984. Food, Sex, and Pollution: A New Guinea Religion. Rutgers University Press, New Brunswick, N.J.

Pelchat, M. L., and P. Rozin. 1982. The special role of nausea in the acquisition of food dislikes by humans. Appetite 3:341-351.

Petó, E. 1936. Contribution to the development of smell feeling. Br. J. Med. Psychol. 15:314-320.

Pliner, P. 1982. The effects of mere exposure on liking for edible substances. Appetite 3:283-290.

Pliner, P., P. Rozin, M. Cooper, and G. Woody. In press. The minimal role of specific post-ingestional effects in the acquisition of liking for foods. Appetite.

Rozin, P. 1978. The use of characteristic flavorings in human culinary practice. Pp. 101-127 in C. M. Apt, ed. Flavor: Its Chemical, Behavioral, and Commercial Aspects. Westview Press, Boulder, Colo.

Rozin, P. 1982. Human food selection: The interaction of biology, culture and individual experience. Pp. 225-254 in L. M. Barker, ed. The Psychobiology of Human Food Selection. AVI, Bridgeport, Conn.

Rozin, P., and A. E. Fallon. 1980. The psychological categorization of foods and non-foods: A preliminary taxonomy of food rejections. Appetite 1:193-201.

Rozin, P., and A. E. Fallon. 1981. The acquisition of likes and dislikes for foods. Pp. 35-48 in J. Solms and R. L. Hall, eds. Criteria of Food Acceptance: How Man Chooses What He Eats. A Symposium. Forster, Zurich.

Rozin, P., and A. E. Fallon. 1985. That's disgusting! Psychology Today 19(7):60-63.

Rozin, P., and J. W. Kalat. 1971. Specific hungers and poison avoidance as adaptive specializations of learning. Psychol. Rev. 78:459-486.

Rozin, P., and D. Schiller. 1980. The nature and acquisition of a preference for chili pepper by humans. Motiv. Emot. 4:77-101.

Rozin, P., L. Gruss, and G. Berk. 1979. The reversal of innate aversions: Attempts to induce a preference for chili peppers in rats. J. Comp. Physiol. Psychol. 93:1001-1014.

Rozin, P., L. Ebert, and J. Schull. 1982. Some like it hot: A temporal analysis of hedonic responses to chili pepper. Appetite 3:13-22.

Rozin, P., L. Hammer, H. Oster, T. Horowitz, and V. MarMora. In press. The child's conception of food: Differentiation of categories of rejected substances in the 1.4 to 5 year age range. Appetite.

Senn, M. J. E., and A. J. Solnit. 1968. Problems in Child Behavior and Development. Lea and Febiger, Philadelphia, Pa.

Solomon, R. L. 1980. The opponent-process theory of acquired motivation. Am. Psychol. 35:691-712.

Stang, D. J. 1975. When familiarity breeds contempt, absence makes the heart grow fonder: Effects of exposure and delay on taste pleasantness ratings. Bull. Psychon. Soc. 6:273-275.

Zahorik, D. 1979. Learned changes in preferences for chemical stimuli: Asymmetrical effects of positive and negative consequences, and species differences in learning. Pp. 233-246 in J. H. A. Kroeze, ed. Preference Behavior and Chemoreception. Information Retrieval, London.

Zajonc, R. B. 1968. Attitudinal effects of mere exposure. J. Pers. Soc. Psychol. 9 (Part 2):1-27.

Zellner, D. A., P. Rozin, M. Aron, and C. Kulish. 1983. Conditioned enhancement of humans' liking for flavors by pairing with sweetness. Learn. Motiv. 14:338-350.

Factors That Shape Eating Patterns: A Consumer Behavior Perspective

KENNETH J. ROERING, DAVID M. BOUSH,
and SHANNON H. SHIPP

Eating patterns are affected by a complex set of economic, social, and psychological factors. One approach to understanding these factors is to study consumer behavior—that is, the acts by which persons obtain and use economic goods and services, including the decisions that precede and determine these acts (Block and Roering, 1979). Although its roots can be traced to the great philosophers, economists, and psychological laboratories, consumer-behavior research is only about 30 years old, the most important research having occurred in the last 15 years. When Block and Roering (1976) published their first book on consumer behavior, there were perhaps four or five others available. Today the number of consumer-behavior texts is well into the 50s, and the number of new books is increasing dramatically. This growth in consumer-behavior literature reflects both increased interest and research progress. Unfortunately, this literature is not well known by many groups, such as public policymakers, that might benefit from it.

An understanding of consumer behavior can benefit a variety of users. For example, in marketing, where perhaps the most strongly held tenet is that products must meet consumer needs and desires, consumer research can help marketing managers make decisions regarding product offerings. Or in such areas as consumer protection and consumer education, understanding how consumers behave can aid public policymakers in their decisions.

This paper examines consumer behavior by presenting the various physiological, social, economic, and cognitive perspectives of past consumer behavior research and focusing on the information-processing approach—that is, how consumers acquire, organize, and use information to make consumption choices.

CONSUMER BEHAVIOR THEORIES AND RESEARCH

The Physiological Approach

Since its inception, consumer-behavior research has focused on measures of behavior at the molecular level. Most researchers have attempted to measure some physiological change that occurs when a subject is exposed to a stimulus, such as an advertisement (Krober-Riel, 1979). Although in some cases the magnitude of emotional response could be reliably measured, proponents of this approach were seeking measures (not yet reliably operationalized) of the direction of responses and persuasiveness of the message (Kassarjian, 1982). More specific descriptions of these physiological research approaches are given in the following paragraphs.

Arousal and Activation. The assumption underlying arousal and activation studies is that cognition and behavior originate in physiological processes. Several authors, however, have documented the noncorrespondence between measures of arousal and verbal responses (Bettman, 1979; Russo, 1978). Measures of activation, such as electroencephalograph studies, show promise for the analysis of basic cognitive processes, but they are expensive and difficult to apply to large samples.

Eye Movement, Skin Response, and Voice Analysis. Results from studies using galvanic skin response, pupil dilation, and voice pitch analysis to measure consumer response have not been very useful in predicting aspects of consumer behavior (Bettman, 1979). Although data of high validity have sometimes been obtained in eye movement studies, they are expensive to obtain. Moreover, because of the time and equipment required to test each subject, the method is not feasible for large sample sizes.

Brain Hemisphere Lateralization. Recently, the implications of hemispheric lateralization have attracted some interest (see, for example, Weinstein, 1980). Activities associated with the left side of the brain have been described as analytical and logical, and those associated with the right side as nonverbal, pictorial, and integrative (McCallum and Glynn, 1979). Research in this area has not yet been developed to the point that results can be applied to consumer behavior.

The Social Approach

Social theories of consumer behavior emphasize the importance of other people in shaping a person's behavior. Some authors suggest that the appropriate unit of analysis for much consumer behavior is the family rather than the person. For example, Davis and Rigaux (1974) examined the family decision-making process and found that wives seem to dominate in decisions about food products. Other researchers focused on children and consumer socialization (Adler *et al.*, 1980; Ward and Wackman, 1974) and interpersonal influence (Churchill and Moschis, 1979). These social forces can also be integrated in the cognitive approach to analyzing consumer behavior (see below).

The Economic Psychology Approach

Economic psychology developed as a reaction to traditional economics. Katona (1951, 1975) has substantially modified many predictions relating individual behavior to macroeconomic variables. For example, traditional economics predicts that when people expect prices to go up they save less and spend more. In contrast, Katona showed that people feel pessimistic when they face inflation and delay the purchase of discretionary items so that more money will be available for necessities (Katona, 1951).

Interest in economic psychology has waned somewhat in the United States, but continues at a lively rate in Europe under the direction of such researchers as Reynaud (1984), Warneryd (1980), and Van Veldhoven (1980).

The Learning Theory Approach

In the behaviorist school, which dominated American psychology from the 1940s through the early 1970s, discussion of cognitive processes was believed to be too ''mentalistic'' to be useful because only behavioral hypotheses could be empirically tested (Lachman *et al.*, 1979). Learning theorists viewed complex behaviors as aggregations of much smaller units of behavior for which a person had been reinforced. Reinforcement led to perseverance of a behavior, whereas lack of reinforcement caused the behavior to become extinguished (Hill, 1977). Although reinforcement is implicit in most consumer-behavior theories, the need to consider complex cognitive processes is generally acknowledged (Assael, 1984).

The Cognitive Approach

Attitude Research. In the past 20 years, an enormous amount of literature has been written on attitude—i.e., a person's predisposition to behave in a particular way (Loudon and Della Bitta, 1979). Much of this research focused on attitude change and on prediction of behavior from attitudes. For example, Fishbein and Ajzen (1975) developed, with considerable research effort, the multiattribute model of evaluation, which predicted a consumer's evaluation of a product (the attitude object) by a summation, across attributes, of the importance of each attribute multiplied by the belief that the product contained that attribute.

The extended Fishbein attitude-behavior model predicted a behavior from the person's attitude toward the behavior rather than just from the attitude toward the object of the behavior (Fishbein and Ajzen, 1975). The attitude toward a behavior is influenced by whether the person feels that significant other people approve of the behavior. For example, adopting a strict vegetarian diet is predicted by a person's attitudes toward vegetarianism rather than by attitudes toward vegetables. These attitudes, in turn, are affected by one's perceptions of approval of vegetarianism by significant persons in one's life.

Cognitive Response. The assumption in cognitive response research is that persuasive communications evoke thoughts that mediate attitude change (Petty, 1977). When incoming information conflicts with a person's beliefs, counterarguments are likely to be generated, and the credibility of the information source may be derogated (see Cialdini *et al.*, 1981, and Petty *et al.*, 1980, for reviews).

Information Processing. For the past 10 to 15 years, information processing has been the dominant approach in consumer-behavior research. A major assumption of this approach is that the ability of humans to consider all possible decision alternatives and to reach a utility-maximizing decision is limited. Instead, the choice process is characterized by bounded rationality (March and Simon, 1958) in which persons consider or process only a limited amount of the information available for decision making. The resulting decision is satisfying rather than optimizing. The computer has played an important role in information processing; many of the concepts have resulted from attempts to model human intelligence with a computer. Since information processing is currently the most dominant perspective in consumer behavior research, it is discussed in much greater detail below.

INFORMATION PROCESSING

Information processing focuses on the mechanisms of cognition: attention, perception, and memory. That is, it focuses on the factors that are the basis of a behavior rather than on the behavior itself. Consumer-behavior models that use information processing do not ignore learning effects; rather, they go beyond simple behavioral predictions to achieve more complex explanations of consumer behavior. The information-processing approach interprets consumer choices as a function of three processes: information acquisition, information organization, and information utilization. Figure 1 presents these three processes in a simplified form.

Information acquired from external sources, as well as information recalled from memory, affects consumer behavior. If external information is to influence consumer choice, it must be perceived, represented in memory, and then organized so that the consumer can gain access to it when necessary. For example, Bettman and Kakkar (1979) showed that consumers tend to organize information regarding familiar products by brand. The consumer's personal characteristics, such as age, social class, and personal life-style, affect the way this information is organized (Capon and Burke, 1980; Henry, 1980).

When making a product choice, consumers gain access to the organized information in their memory by using various decision rules. In a routine purchase situation, little information may be retrieved, and the consumer may invoke a simple decision rule, such as "buy the same brand as last time." In a more important purchase situation, consumers may attempt

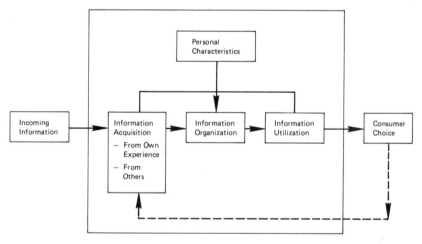

FIGURE 1   Overview of information processing. Adapted from Sternthal and Craig, 1982.

to recall all the pertinent information stored in their memory, actively search for more information, and then use a complicated decision rule, such as comparing alternatives on a range of dimensions. The consumer's choice will affect future choices, as shown in Figure 1. (The arrow leading from consumer choice back to information acquisition suggests that how a choice is reinforced will influence future choices.)

Information Acquisition

Figure 2 presents a more detailed representation of information acquisition. A consumer actively processes incoming information in four stages: exposure to information, information reception, cognitive analysis, and attitude formation. Each stage is influenced by long-term memory.

Exposure to information can be either active or passive and can be affected by a consumer's judgment of the information's usefulness. A consumer on a strict weight reduction diet may actively search for information about a food's caloric content. To a consumer who is less concerned about weight reduction, caloric content information may not be actively sought.

Information reception involves sensory arousal and attention. Research indicates that in order for a consumer to attend to information, a moderate

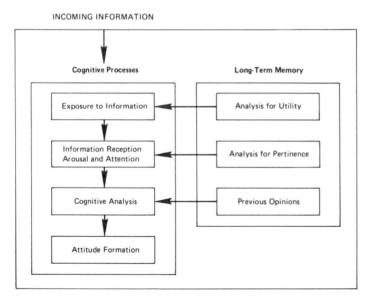

FIGURE 2   The information acquisition process. Adapted from Sternthal and Craig, 1982.

level of arousal is optimal, whereas a high level limits breadth of attention and a low level limits depth of attention (Hansen, 1972). Consumers are selective about the information that receives their attention: It must be pertinent and have a signal strong enough to arouse them.

Cognitive analysis is required for information to influence a consumer's choice. Initially, the information must be comprehended; that is, the consumer determines the extent to which the meaning inferred from the message is the same as that intended by the source. Once the message is received, the consumer retrieves from memory thoughts relevant to the object or issue and evaluates them in relation to the message. A judgment is then made about the message, based on its integration with previously held opinion. If the previously held opinion differs from the present message, consumers generate counterarguments that impede message acceptance. If the previously held opinion is consistent with the new information, consumers more readily accept the present message.

Information Organization

Once the information is acquired, it must be organized in a meaningful way in memory to facilitate utilization. Researchers have found that consumers organize information by brand, by attribute, or by some combination of the two (Bettman and Kakkar, 1977; Biehal and Chakravarti, 1982). Consumers prefer different means of organizing information under different conditions. A consumer's familiarity with the product, for example, is one variable that affects the preferred method of organizing information about that product (Johnson and Russo, 1984; Park and Lessig, 1981). If consumers are familiar with a product class, they prefer to organize incoming information by brand. If consumers are less familiar with the product class, they seem to prefer organization of incoming information by attribute.

Information Utilization

Consumers employ heuristics (empirical rules of thumb) to facilitate making a satisfactory choice with minimum effort. Four models describe the use of these heuristics by consumers: the linear model, the lexicographic model, the conjunctive model, and the disjunctive model. (For a complete description of the four models, see Bettman, 1979.)

Linear Model.   Most investigations of information organization have tested the extent to which the linear model predicts preference. All linear models assume that two components account for a consumer's judgment:

(1) belief that an alternative (a potential product choice) possesses some attribute and (2) evaluation of that attribute's importance. In a typical product judgment, a consumer decides the importance of each product attribute, evaluates the extent to which a product possesses each attribute, multiplies the importance weights by the attribute evaluations, and sums across all attributes. For example, a consumer who is judging loaves of bread might decide that fiber content and freshness are the most important attributes in evaluating different brands. To use the model, the consumer assigns weights to these attributes based on their importance to the purchase decision and evaluates each brand's degree of fiber content and freshness. To derive a score for each brand, the consumer multiplies the two attributes weighted by their importance scores and the score of each brand on each attribute. The consumer selects the brand with the highest score.

A basic feature of the linear model is that it views decision making as a compensatory process. That is, a low evaluation of a product on one attribute can be overcome by a high evaluation on another attribute. The linear model makes reasonably accurate predictions, especially when few attributes are used in making judgments. However, consumers' explanations of their own decision-making processes do not fit the linear model. In addition, when consumers are asked to apply various models consciously to the selection of products, they find the linear model difficult to use (Russ, 1971; Sheridan et al., 1975).

The Lexicographic Model. The lexicographic model involves a sequential evaluation that simplifies choice (Bettman, 1979). The decision maker compares alternative products by the most important attribute. If one product is superior on that attribute, it is chosen; if no product is superior, the products are then compared on the second most important attribute. The process continues until an alternative is chosen. For example, the consumer in the bread-purchasing example may rank freshness as the most important and fiber content as the second most important product attribute. If none of the alternative loaves is noticeably most fresh, the loaf with the highest fiber content, the second most important attribute, would be selected.

The Conjunctive Model. In the conjunctive model, the consumer makes a choice that meets minimum criteria on all relevant attributes. For example, the consumer chooses a loaf of bread that is suitably fresh, contains fiber, and is low in price. Frequently, a second model must be applied because the conjunctive model may not produce a unique choice.

The Disjunctive Model.   The disjunctive model is often used to reduce the number of acceptable alternative products. As with the conjunctive model, a minimum acceptable level is determined for each attribute. However, the alternative products selected are those that surpass the minimum level on any attribute.

Consumers can and do use the decision rules from more than one of the above models to make a product choice. They may use a disjunctive rule to narrow the set of alternatives, a conjunctive rule to limit that set further, and then a linear or lexicographic rule to make the final choice.

Thus, no decision model is best; rather, each is used under different circumstances, depending on decision complexity, perceived risk, and the format in which information is presented. Decision complexity increases with the number of possible alternatives, the number of attribute dimensions, and the novelty of the choice situation.

Nutrition Information Processing

Information Acquisition.   In several survey studies (Daly, 1976; cf. Rudell, 1979), consumers reported a desire for more nutrition information, contending that they would use it. Laboratory studies, however, do not support those reports. In a series of experiments, Jacoby *et al.* (1977) found that only one-third of their subjects searched for such information in making choices related to nutrition. Furthermore, many consumers have poor knowledge of nutrition. In a recent survey (Clydesdale, 1984), only 4 of 700 students were aware of the nitrate issue, and two of those seemed to understand it.

Information Misuse and Misunderstanding.   Consumers often misunderstand nutrition information. If they do understand it, they tend to misuse it. Several authors (Daly, 1976; Jacoby *et al.*, 1977) reported poor nutrition information comprehension among subjects with varied demographic characteristics and low scores on tests of nutrition knowledge among college undergraduates. Consumers do not understand the implications of nutrient composition of foods or adherence to a particular diet. Asam and Bucklin (1973) found that subjects rated products as more nutritious when information on nutritional content was printed on the package than when the same products were presented with less information on the package. Proprietary studies indicate that some consumers interpret the absence of particular ingredients, such as caffeine and sugar, as indicators of product quality. In short, consumers assess the nutritional content of food using, at best, inadequate information; moreover, they apply inaccurate, simplifying heuristic rules to make their product choices.

Limits to Information Processing. The notion that people are limited in their capacity to process information is a basic assumption of information processing. One implication of this assumption is that consumers can experience information overload (Jacoby, 1984; Jacoby *et al.*, 1974), a condition that seriously inhibits information processing and results in less-effective consumer decision making.

Improving Information Processing. The ability of consumers to process nutrition information can be improved. When product information is presented in a manner consistent with the way similar information is organized in the consumer's memory, considerably less effort is required for the person to process it adequately. Scammon (1977) reported that consumers understood and used nutrition information more when it was presented descriptively than when the same information was presented as Recommended Dietary Allowances (RDAs) (NRC, 1980). Descriptive presentation of nutrition information, however, may have the disadvantage of imprecision.

Future Research

The information-processing approach to consumer behavior has produced some useful insights. Many questions remain, however, and the following priorities for future research are suggested to help answer those questions.

• Develop methods to increase consumer attention to nutrition information.

• Develop methods to enhance consumers' understanding and use of nutrition information. Particularly needed is exploration of various decision rules, including the circumstances under which consumers use different rules.

• Determine the limits on the consumer's capacity to process nutrition information. The amount of information that can be adequately processed appears to depend on the context of the situation. Therefore, researchers should establish the optimum amounts of presented information for various situations.

• Determine how use context and purchase context affect processing of nutrition information. That is, information may be processed differently, depending on whether a food is consumed as a meal or a snack and whether it is consumed by family, self, or guests. Also, consumers may use different decision rules when ordering food in a restaurant than when buying food in a supermarket.

• Determine nutrition information needs of various consumer groups, particularly those at nutritional risk. Goals in making choices pertaining to nutrition differ for various groups. Some consumers may, for example, require more detailed specification of fiber, sugar, or vitamin content than do others.

CONCLUDING COMMENT

Nutritionists and other researchers agree on the importance of improving the American diet and monitoring nutritional intake. However, rather than simply describing nutritional problems, relevant theory should be applied to solving them. Studying consumer behavior and, more specifically, consumer information processing can improve our understanding of how nutritional choices are made. To date, research has shown that consumers do not adequately obtain or comprehend nutrition information and that the information they do understand is often misused. A research agenda that focuses on information processing, such as that proposed here, could ultimately help consumers make better nutritional choices.

REFERENCES

Adler, R. P., S. Ward, G. S. Lesser, L. K. Meringoff, T. S. Robertson, and J. R. Rossiter. 1980. The Effect of Television Advertising on Children: Review and Recommendations. Lexington Books, Lexington, Mass.

Asam, E. H., and L. P. Bucklin. 1973. Nutritional labeling for canned goods: A study of consumer response. J. Mark. 37:32-37.

Assael, H. 1984. Consumer Behavior and Marketing Action. Kent, New York.

Bettman, J. 1979. An Information Processing Theory of Consumer Choice. Addison Wesley, Reading, Mass.

Bettman, J., and P. Kakkar. 1977. Effects of information presentation format on consumer information acquisition strategies. J. Consum. Res. 3:233-240.

Biehal, G., and D. Chakravarti. 1982. Information presentation format as determinants of consumers' memory retrieval and choice processes. J. Consum. Res. 8:431-441.

Block, C. E., and K. J. Roering. 1976. Essentials of Consumer Behavior, 1st ed. The Dryden Press, Hinsdale, Ill.

Block, C. E., and K. J. Roering. 1979. Essentials of Consumer Behavior, 2nd ed. The Dryden Press, Hinsdale, Ill.

Capon, N., and M. Burke. 1980. Individual, product class, and task-related factors in consumer information processing. J. Consum. Res. 7:314-326.

Churchill, G. A., and G. P. Moschis. 1979. Television and interpersonal influences on adolescent consumer learning. J. Consum. Res. 6:23-35.

Cialdini, R. B., R. E. Petty, and J. T. Cacioppo. 1981. Attitude and attitude change. Annu. Rev. Psychol. 32:348-404.

Clydesdale, F. M. 1984. Culture, fitness, and health. Food Technol. 38(11):108-111.

Daly, P. A. 1976. The response of consumers to nutritional labeling. J. Consum. Affairs 10:170-178.

Davis, H. L., and B. P. Rigaux. 1974. Perception of mental roles in decision processes. J. Consum. Res. 1:51-62.

Fishbein, M., and I. Ajzen. 1975. Belief, Attitude, Intention, and Behavior. Addison-Wesley, Reading, Mass.

Hansen, F. 1972. Consumer Choice Behavior: A Cognitive Theory. New York Free Press, New York.

Henry, W. 1980. The effect of information processing ability on processing accuracy. J. Consum. Res. 7:42-48.

Hill, W. F. 1977. Learning: A Survey of Psychological Interpretations. Harper and Row, New York.

Jacoby, J. 1984. Perspective on information overload. J. Consum. Res. 10:432-435.

Jacoby, J., D. E. Speller, and C. A. Kohn. 1974. Brand choice behavior as a function of information load. J. Mark. Res. 11:63-69.

Jacoby, J., R. W. Chestnut, and W. Silberman. 1977. Consumer use and comprehension of nutritional information. J. Consum. Res. 4:119-128.

Johnson, E., and J. E. Russo. 1984. Product familiarity and learning new information. J. Consum. Res. 11:542-550.

Kassarjian, H. H. 1982. Consumer psychology. Annu. Rev. Psychol. 33:619-649.

Katona, G. 1951. Psychological Analysis of Economic Behavior. McGraw-Hill, New York.

Katona, G. 1975. Psychological Economics. Elsevier, Amsterdam.

Krober-Riel, W. 1979. Activation research: Psychobiological Approaches in Consumer Research. J. Consum. Res. 5:240-250.

Lachman, R., J. Lachman, and E. Butterfield. 1979. Cognitive Psychology and Information Processing: An Introduction. Erlbaum, Hillsdale, N.J.

Loudon, D. L., and A. J. Della Bitta. 1979. Consumer Behavior: Concepts and Applications. McGraw-Hill, New York.

March, J. G., and H. A. Simon. 1958. Organizations. Wiley, New York.

McCallum, A. S., and S. A. Glynn. 1979. Hemispheric specialization and creative behavior. J. Creat. Behav. 13:263-273.

NRC (National Research Council). 1980. Recommended Dietary Allowances, 9th ed. A report of the Food and Nutrition Board, Assembly of Life Sciences. National Academy of Sciences, Washington, D.C.

Park, C. W., and P. V. Lessig. 1981. Familiarity and its impact on consumer decision biases and heuristics. J. Consum. Res. 8:223-230.

Petty, R. E. 1977. The importance of cognitive responses in persuasion. Adv. Consum. Res. 4:357-362.

Petty, R. E., T. Ostrum, and T. Brock, eds. 1980. Cognitive Responses in Persuasion. Erlbaum, Hillsdale, N.J.

Reynaud, P. L. 1984. Précis de Psychologie Economique. Presses Université de France, Paris.

Rudell, E. 1979. Consumer Food Selection and Nutrition Information. Praeger, New York.

Russ, F. A. 1971. Consumer Evaluation of Alternative Product Models. Ph.D. dissertation, Carnegie-Mellon University.

Russo, J. E. 1978. Eye fixations can save the world: A critical evaluation and a comparison between eye fixations and other information processing methodologies. Adv. Consum. Res. 561-570.

Scammon, D. L. 1977. Information load and consumers. Consum. Res. 4:148-155.

Sheridan, J. E., M. D. Richards, and J. W. Slocum. 1975. Comparative analysis of expectancy and heuristic models of decision behavior. J. Appl. Psychol. 60:361-368.

Sternthal, B., and C. S. Craig. 1982. Consumer Behavior: An Information Processing Perspective. Prentice-Hall, Englewood Cliffs, N.J.

Van Veldhoven, G. M. 1980. Psychological Aspects of Taxation. Presented at the 5th Am. Colloq. Eur. Econ. Psychol., Leuven, Belgium.

Ward, S., and D. B. Wackman. 1974. Children's information processing of television advertising. Pp. 119-146 in P. Clarke, ed. New Models for Communication Research. Sage, Beverly Hills, Calif.

Warneryd, K. E. 1980. Taxes and Economic Behavior. Presented at the 5th Am. Colloq. Eur. Econ. Psychol., Leuven, Belgium.

Weinstein, S. 1980. Brain wave analysis in attitude research: Past, present and future. Pp. 41-47 in R. W. Olshavsky, ed. Attitude Research Enters the 80's. American Marketing Association, Chicago, Ill.

III
Eating Trends and
Nutritional Consequences

Introduction

HELEN A. GUTHRIE

In this session, two previously unpublished studies are presented: an analysis of variety in the diet and an analysis of snacking and eating away from home. The 1977-1978 Nationwide Food Consumption Survey (NFCS) (USDA, 1983, 1984) and the Health and Nutrition Examination Surveys (HANES I and NHANES II) (USDHEW, 1979, 1984) have provided insights into the eating trends of Americans and the resulting nutritional adequacy of their diets (Crocetti and Guthrie, 1982). Some results from those analyses confirmed commonly held beliefs about how Americans eat. Other results, however, were surprising and brought into question long-held assumptions about eating trends in the United States. These findings are briefly presented here.

NFCS AND HANES

Since their inception, both NFCS and HANES have provided information on the food and nutrient intake of the U.S. population. In order to use the findings of the early surveys for nutritional guidance, nutrition intervention programs, and food and agricultural policy, it became obvious that information beyond what Americans eat was needed; for example, we needed information on social, economic, demographic, and cultural factors associated with varying food patterns.

Therefore, the 1977-1978 NFCS was modified to provide data sufficient to identify and determine the nutritional consequences of various eating patterns of persons and to identify the demographic characteristics of

87

respondents with common patterns of nutritional adequacy and inadequacy. Similarly, NHANES II collected sufficient additional information on health practices to permit inferences about health nutrition indicators.

Meal Patterns

The NFCS indicated that 90% of all respondents ate regular meals—that is, two or three meals each day for 3 consecutive days (Crocetti and Guthrie, 1982). Of these, two-thirds ate three meals on each of 3 days, 8% ate two meals on each of 3 days, and the remaining respondents ate two or three meals on each of 3 days. The nutritional adequacy of respondents' diets was directly related to the number of days that respondents consumed regular meals, regardless of the number of snacks. Almost 50% of those who regularly ate two meals per day skipped breakfast, whereas when others missed a meal, it was more often the midday meal than breakfast. When the meal pattern differed for one day, that day was almost invariably a weekend day. The classification of eating occasion was based on the respondent's designation of breakfast, lunch, supper, snack, and so on.

Snacking

Three-quarters of the NFCS respondents reported snacking at least once in 3 days. When their intakes were compared to appropriate Recommended Dietary Allowances, those who snacked had more nutritionally adequate diets than those who did not snack, and as the number of snacks increased, the adequacy of diets of all age groups increased. This finding suggests that the nutrient density of snack foods was as high as that of foods selected for meals. For most people who snacked, the snacks provided from 10% to 20% of calories and of 10 assessed nutrients. Traditional snack foods, such as pretzels, chips, and soft drinks, were eaten more often as part of a meal than as a snack; candy and ice cream were the only two foods mentioned more often as snacks than as part of a meal. As anticipated, the frequency of snacking declined with age.

Compliance with Nutritional Guidance

The NFCS data were analyzed to determine the extent to which respondents chose foods that conformed to the basic four food guidance approach—the major nutrition education effort at the time of the survey (Crocetti and Guthrie, 1982; Guthrie and Wright, 1984). At least one-half the number of recommended servings from each of the four food groups was consumed by 83% of respondents during the 3-day period, whereas only 3% consumed the recommended 6 servings from both the meat and milk groups and 12 servings from both the cereal and the fruit and vegetable groups. The higher the degree of compliance with the basic four recommendations, the more adequate the diet; however, respondents who followed the food pattern did not necessarily show a recommended distribution of caloric intake from carbohydrates, fat, and protein.

Food Choice

Although grocery stores reportedly stock several thousand food items and the USDA tables of food composition contain well over 4,000 entries, NFCS respondents reported a relatively small number of these foods with any frequency (Guthrie and Wright, 1984). For instance, oranges and orange juice, apples, and bananas accounted for 62% of the mentions of fruits; potatoes, tomatoes, lettuce, beans, peas, and corn accounted for 73% of the mentions of vegetables. Similarly, data from both NHANES and NFCS showed that more than 80% of the assessed nutrients came from fewer than six different foods. In addition, some foods reported in the NFCS were clearly identified with either children or adults (Crocetti and Guthrie, 1982). For example, milk, ice cream, soft drinks, and nut butters were consumed more frequently by children than by adults, whereas eggs and cheese were consumed more by adults. Tea and coffee, reported an average of 5.27 times over a 3-day period, were the most frequently reported items, followed closely by milk (5.1 mentions) and bread (4.7 mentions). This information should provide a basis for developing a less burdensome approach to assessing dietary intake and adequacy.

Data from the NFCS and NHANES are voluminous, and nutritionists must continue to study them in order to answer questions about relationships among food patterns, nutrient adequacy, health indicators, and social factors. The following two papers analyze data from the NFCS that relate to variety in the diet and to snacking and eating away from home; such analyses provide a better understanding of the complexities of American eating patterns and a stronger foundation on which to base nutrition policies and education efforts.

REFERENCES

Crocetti, A. F., and H. A. Guthrie. 1982. Eating Behavior and Associated Nutrient Quality of Diets. Final report for contract 53-22 U4-9-192, October. Human Nutrition Center, Science and Education Administration. U.S. Department of Agriculture, Washington, D.C.

Guthrie, H. A., and H. S. Wright. 1984. Assessing Dietary Intakes. Final report for contract

58-3198-2-57, December. Human Nutrition Information Center. U.S. Department of Agriculture, Washington, D.C.

USDA (U.S. Department of Agriculture). 1983. Food Intakes: Individuals in 48 States, Year 1977-78. Human Nutrition Information Service, Consumer Nutrition Division, Nationwide Food Consumption Survey 1977-78, Report No. I-1, August. U.S. Department of Agriculture, Hyattsville, Md.

USDA (U.S. Department of Agriculture). 1984. Food Intakes: Individuals in 48 States, Year 1977-78. Human Nutrition Information Service, Consumer Nutrition Division, Nationwide Food Consumption Survey 1977-78, Report No. I-2, November. U.S. Department of Agriculture, Hyattsville, Md.

USDHEW (U.S. Department of Health, Education, and Welfare). 1979. Dietary Intake Source Data: United States, 1971-74. DHEW Publication No. (PHS) 79-1221. Public Health Service, Office of Health Research, Statistics, and Technology. National Center for Health Statistics, Hyattsville, Md.

USDHHS (U.S. Department of Health and Human Services). 1984. Dietary Intake Source Data: United States, 1976-80. DHEW Publication No. (PHS) 83-1681. Public Health Service, Office of Health Research, Statistics, and Technology. National Center for Health Statistics, Hyattsville, Md.

Snacking and Eating Away from Home

KAREN J. MORGAN and BASILE GOUNGETAS

Affluence, changes in lifestyle, greater employment of women, smaller households, increased accessibility to commercial food establishments, and increased availability of highly processed foods have influenced the U.S. population's food consumption patterns. Some researchers believe that these factors have led to overconsumption of such dietary components as fat, cholesterol, refined carbohydrate, and sodium (Abrams, 1978; Bunch and Hall, 1983). Overconsumption of these components may be linked with many health problems now prevalent in the United States, according to the U.S. Department of Agriculture and the U.S. Department of Health, Education, and Welfare (USDA and USDHEW, 1980).

In addition to overconsumption is the problem of nutrient deficiency. Both the National Health and Examination Survey II (NHANES II) and the Nationwide Food Consumption Survey (NFCS) have identified calcium and iron as "problem nutrients"—nutrients not consumed at levels equivalent to the National Research Council's (NRC) Recommended Dietary Allowances (RDAs) (NRC, 1980) for all age-sex groups. The NFCS has also indicated that magnesium and vitamin B_6 may be problem nutrients (Carroll et al., 1983; USDA, 1984). The extent to which the reported average low-level intakes reflect a national health threat is difficult to determine; however, it is prudent to monitor continually estimated intake levels of problem nutrients and associated food consumption patterns.

Although the per capita caloric consumption of U.S. residents has remained roughly the same as that 70 years ago (Bogart et al., 1973), eating patterns have changed dramatically during the same period. For example,

Pao and Mickle (1980) established that 59% to 70% of U.S. children and teenagers had at least one snack per day. Similar snacking frequencies for children and teenagers have been reported by other researchers (Bundy *et al.*, 1982; Cala *et al.*, 1981). Pao and Mickle (1980) also reported that adults snacked less frequently than children and teenagers; 40% to 64% of the surveyed adults consumed at least one snack per day. Another change in the U.S. population's food consumption patterns is the increase in food eaten away from home. The percentage of the food dollar spent on away-from-home food consumption increased from 27% in 1960 to more than 33% in 1970, and it is expected to exceed 40% by the mid-1980s (Putnam and Van Dress, 1984). Utilizing the NFCS, Guenther and Chandler (1980) reported that 44% of the total sample consumed some food away from home on the day surveyed.

Research continues to identify food consumption patterns of the U.S. population and to relate these patterns to nutrient intake levels. Another research effort concentrates on the elucidation of relationships between diet and the development and progression of chronic, degenerative diseases. For example, cardiovascular disease, hypertension, and various cancers have been linked to dietary intake patterns (Kornitzer *et al.*, 1979; McGill, 1979; McGill and Mott, 1976; Pooling Project Research Group, 1978; Shekelle *et al.*, 1981). If demographic and lifestyle trends can be linked to significant changes in food consumption patterns, and the associated dietary intake differences can be linked to the incidence of chronic diseases, then implications of nutrition education and research programs will have more direct effects on food and health policy.

METHODS

This study explored two specific eating patterns: snacking and consuming meals away from home. Both eating patterns were evaluated by the same methods. Thus, a detailed description of methods used to study snack consumption is provided, followed by a brief description of the methods used to assess away-from-home meal consumption.

Data

Three-day dietary records from USDA's NFCS were used for this investigation. The NFCS methodology has been described at length elsewhere (USDA, 1980). For the present study, the sample was screened so that only persons aged 1 year and older who had complete 3-day records, including specification of kind of eating occasion and place of food obtainment, were included. Weights were deemed unreliable after the screening and were not used; the resultant sample size was 27,322 unweighted persons. Intakes of food energy, fat, cholesterol, sodium, total sugar, calcium, vitamin B_6, iron, and magnesium were calculated from the intake data by using the Michigan State University (MSU) Nutrient Data Bank (Morgan and Zabik, 1983). The relationship between the USDA Nutrient Data Bank and the MSU Nutrient Data Bank has been described in detail by Fischer *et al.* (in press).

Although the unit of observation was the person, some of the variables in the analyses were specified at the household level. Therefore, persons were matched with households to identify the necessary household characteristics. The personal characteristics used in the analysis were age and sex. Also included in the analysis were season of the year and day of the week when the intake data were collected.

Analyses

Snacking Patterns.   To assess patterns of snack consumption, the sample was partitioned by the numbers of snacks a person reported consuming during the 3 surveyed days. These partitions were zero, one to three, four to six, seven to nine, and ten or more snacks. Ordinary least-squares regressions were used to identify the snackers (SASI, 1982). Estimated regression coefficients for each of the selected personal and household characteristics were determined by using the number of snacks consumed during 3 surveyed days as the dependent variable. These regressions were estimated for the total sample and for each of 12 age-sex groups: males and females (aged 1 to 6 years and 7 to 12 years), males (aged 13 to 18 years, 19 to 24 years, 25 to 44 years, 45 to 64 years, and 65 years and older), and females (aged 13 to 18 years, 19 to 24 years, 25 to 44 years, 45 to 64 years, and 65 years and older). To evaluate the resulting coefficient estimates, t-statistics were used (SASI, 1982).

The independent variables in the regressions were selected and evaluated as follows. Per capita annual income was hypothesized to have a positive relationship with snack consumption. The per capita annual income levels were partitioned into six groups: $999 or less, $1,000 to $3,999, $4,000 to $6,999, $7,000 to $9,999, $10,000 to $16,999, and $17,000 or more. Unfortunately, 6,622 persons did not report income; therefore, analyses with the income variable were restricted to 20,700 persons. Household size was hypothesized to have an inverse relationship with snack consumption, i.e., members of small households are less likely to consistently prepare and consume complete meals. The sample partitions for household size were one, two, three, four, five, and six or more persons per household. The independent variables of age and sex were included in the regression analyses to reflect changing nutritional requirements and as proxies for age-related food consumption patterns. It was hypothesized that children and teenagers snack more frequently than adults.

Head of household was identified as dual, male only, or female only and was used as a proxy for family composition. Households with one head were assumed to contain persons who snack more because regular meals are likely to be less organized. Education level of household head(s) was used as a proxy for nutrition knowledge and ability to make informed food choices. The education variable included two categories: less than high school education and high school education or more. Employment of household heads, specified as employed or not employed, was incorporated as a proxy for the opportunity cost of time.

Degree of urbanization and region of the country where persons resided were included in the regressions as proxies for lifestyle and differing availabilities of foods. Persons who reside in suburban and central city areas are believed to snack more because of the accessibility of food stores and fast-food outlets. There was no basis for anticipating differences in snacking due to region of country, but this variable was included to control for possible interregional price effects. Because snack consumption is believed to be higher on weekend days than on weekdays, the day of the week on which intake data were collected was reflected in the specified regressions. It was also hypothesized that more snacking may occur in summer months than in other seasons because eating schedules are generally less routine during this period, especially for children and teenagers.

The impact of snack consumption on diet quality was assessed by calculating the average daily intake of selected dietary components for groups of people classified by age and sex as well as by the number of snacks consumed during 3 surveyed days. The percentages of total daily intake of each dietary component obtained from foods consumed as snacks were also calculated.

Away-from-Home Eating Patterns. The methods used to determine what kind of person ate various numbers of meals away from home were similar to those used for identifying snackers. That is, ordinary least-squares regressions were determined, with number of meals consumed away from home during 3 surveyed days (i.e., zero, one to two, three to four, five to six, and seven or more meals) as the dependent variable. The independent variables were the same as those for snackers. Average nutrient intake levels were calculated for groups classified by age and sex as well as by number of meals consumed away from home during 3 surveyed days.

In summary, it was hypothesized that households of smaller size and those with higher per capita income consume more meals away from home. Employment of household heads (particularly female household heads), single household heads, and degree of urbanization were anticipated to have a positive relationship with away-from-home food consumption.

Combined Effects of Snacking and Eating Away from Home. Regression analyses were also conducted to determine combined effects of snacking and consuming meals away from home. The proportion of caloric intake obtained from consumed snacks was the dependent variable; independent variables were the same as those in previously described regression analyses but with an additional dummy variable for away-from-home meal consumption. Persons were considered away-from-home meal consumers if they consumed three or more meals away from home during the 3 surveyed days. Results from this regression indicated the need to investigate further the relationship between snacking and away-from-home meal consumption. This final step in the analysis consisted of partitioning the total sample into away-from-home meal consumers and at-home meal consumers and regressing previously specified explanatory variables on the percentage of total caloric intake obtained from consumed snacks.

RESULTS AND DISCUSSION FOR SNACKING

Identification of Persons Who Snacked

Table 1 provides estimated regression coefficients relating selected household and personal characteristics to numbers of snacks consumed during 3 days surveyed for the total sample and for seven selected age-sex subsamples. Regression results for age-sex subsamples that were not selected for discussion here because of space limitations were similar to those for the ones selected. Although per capita income, household size, and age (total sample regression only) were continuous variables, the remainder of the variables were qualitative and incorporated in the specifications as dummy variables. Qualitative effects for female (total sample regression only), spring quarter, weekdays, dual head of household, less than high school education of household heads, employed household heads, Northeast region, and central city were included in the intercept.

As indicated by the signs for the estimated beta coefficients and the *t*-statistic values in Table 1, increasing per capita income had a positive effect on the numbers of snacks consumed by the total sample and by all age-sex groups. Increasing household size, however, had a negative effect on the numbers of snacks consumed by the total sample and by five of the seven age-sex groups. Within the total sample, age was inversely

TABLE 1 Estimated Regression Coefficients for Per Capita Income, Household Size, Age and Sex of Person, Season of Year and Day of Week for Data Collection, and Selected Socioeconomic Variables as Related to the Number of Snacks Consumed During 3 Surveyed Days

		Explanatory Variables for Snack Consumption*				Season of Year			Weekend	Head of Household	
Sample†	Intercept	Per Capita Income	Household Size	Age	Sex	Summer	Fall	Winter	Days	Male	Female
Total (N = 18,423)	3.766‡ (28.82)§	0.041 (6.66)	-0.107 (-7.42)	-0.011 (-9.13)	0.028 (-0.61)	0.178 (2.85)	-0.099 (-1.64)	-0.054 (-0.89)	-0.074 (-1.14)	-0.103 (-0.79)	-0.602 (-8.28)
7-12 yrs. (N = 2,574)	3.232 (11.21)	0.089 (4.05)	-0.051 (-1.62)			0.116 (0.83)	-0.494 (-3.68)	-0.418 (-3.11)	-0.018 (-0.13)	-0.644 (-1.34)	-0.381 (-2.43)
13-18 yrs., male (N = 1,343)	3.792 (9.43)	0.067 (2.43)	-0.107 (-2.47)			0.047 (0.22)	-0.264 (-1.32)	-0.470 (-2.41)	0.225 (1.11)	0.332 (0.64)	-0.575 (-2.50)
25-44 yrs., male (N = 1,602)	3.147 (7.15)	0.029 (1.96)	-0.095 (-1.52)			-0.037 (-0.15)	0.074 (0.31)	0.261 (1.18)	-0.263 (-1.05)	0.385 (1.06)	-1.03 (-1.62)
≥65 yrs., male (N = 523)	2.770 (4.88)	0.009 (0.39)	0.001 (0.01)			0.549 (1.99)	0.303 (1.16)	0.111 (0.42)	-0.355 (-1.26)	-0.744 (-1.77)	-1.883 (-1.81)
13-18 yrs., female (N = 1,309)	3.445 (9.09)	0.031 (1.10)	0.061 (1.52)			-0.125 (-0.69)	-0.372 (-2.07)	-0.418 (-2.25)	0.261 (1.42)	-0.549 (-0.90)	-0.705 (-3.41)
25-44 yrs., female (N = 2,143)	3.518 (9.21)	0.034 (1.66)	-0.164 (-3.25)			0.146 (0.79)	0.059 (0.34)	0.321 (1.77)	-0.086 (-0.45)	-1.162 (-0.48)	-0.748 (-3.49)
≥65 yrs., female (N = 839)	1.952 (3.62)	0.017 (0.85)	-0.115 (-1.27)			0.285 (1.35)	0.214 (1.10)	0.446 (2.20)	-0.066 (-0.27)	-1.113 (-0.62)	0.378 (1.10)

TABLE 1 Continued

Sample†	Education		Employment		Region			Urbanization	
	M ≥ HS	F ≥ HS	M Not	F Not	NC	S	W	Suburban	Nonmetropolitan
Total (N = 18,423)	0.113 (2.11)	0.467 (8.92)	-0.393 (-5.03)	0.010 (0.21)	-0.262 (-4.13)	-0.913 (-15.38)	0.058 (0.83)	0.587 (10.43)	0.100 (1.75)
7–12 yrs. (N = 2,574)	0.103 (0.91)	0.463 (4.10)	-0.444 (-1.98)	0.093 (0.96)	-0.389 (-2.90)	-0.993 (-7.88)	-0.195 (-1.27)	0.411 (3.35)	-0.073 (-0.59)
13–18 yrs., male (N = 1,343)	0.133 (0.80)	0.481 (2.91)	-0.752 (-2.64)	-0.027 (-0.19)	-0.48 (-2.24)	-1.182 (-6.22)	-0.571 (-2.51)	0.454 (2.49)	0.017 (0.09)
25–44 yrs., male (N = 1,602)	0.103 (0.54)	0.767 (3.48)	0.042 (0.11)	0.323 (1.73)	-0.025 (-0.11)	-1.053 (-4.64)	-0.020 (-0.08)	0.693 (3.26)	0.188 (0.84)
≥65 yrs., male (N = 523)	-0.146 (-0.64)	0.378 (1.55)	0.068 (0.25)	-0.554 (-1.69)	-0.384 (-1.32)	-0.954 (-3.62)	0.640 (2.07)	0.379 (1.50)	0.268 (1.09)
13–18 yrs., female (N = 1,309)	-0.128 (-0.83)	0.530 (3.46)	-0.631 (-2.26)	-0.071 (-0.53)	-0.443 (-2.39)	-0.836 (-4.70)	-0.260 (-1.26)	0.587 (3.48)	0.193 (1.14)
25–44 yrs., female (N = 2,143)	-0.002 (-0.01)	0.128 (0.81)	-0.204 (-0.54)	0.095 (0.67)	0.236 (1.25)	-0.620 (-3.49)	0.447 (2.16)	0.972 (5.86)	0.717 (4.09)
≥65 yrs., female (N = 839)	0.219 (0.85)	0.284 (1.78)	0.512 (1.68)	-0.349 (-1.39)	-0.416 (-1.85)	-0.618 (-3.08)	0.349 (1.45)	0.212 (1.09)	-0.131 (-0.73)

*Variables denoted as follows: M ≥ HS, male educated through high school or beyond; F ≥ HS, female educated through high school or beyond; M Not, male not employed; F Not, female not employed; NC, north central; S, South; W, West.
†Dependent variables are expressed as number of snacks consumed during 3 surveyed days.
‡Values are beta coefficients for independent variables.
§Numbers in parentheses are values of *t*-statistics.

related to numbers of snacks consumed. This finding is consistent with previous analyses (Pao and Mickle, 1980). Coefficients for season of the year showed that only the regressions for the total sample and for elderly males provided consistent results with the hypothesis that more snacking occurs in the summer months. However, children and adolescents did consume significantly fewer snacks during the fall and winter seasons. The numbers of snacks reported were not significantly different for day of the week.

Although snack consumption patterns were not significantly different among persons residing in dual-headed households and in male-headed households, persons residing in female-headed households (except for three age-sex groups) tended to consume significantly fewer snacks. These results are not consistent with the hypothesis that single-headed households snack more frequently, perhaps indicating that snacks serve a social function in households with two heads. The education level of female heads was positively related to numbers of snacks consumed by household members, significantly so in the majority of the age-sex subsamples. If level of education served as a proxy for nutrition knowledge or ability to make appropriate food choices, then snacks were evidently viewed as healthful by educated female household heads. The presence of an unemployed male household head, for the most part, significantly decreased the numbers of snacks consumed. Place of residence influenced the numbers of snacks consumed. Persons residing in the South had significantly fewer snacks than those residing in the Northeast and, to a more limited extent, in the West. Furthermore, persons who resided in suburban areas tended to snack more frequently than those residing in central city and nonmetropolitan areas.

Diet Quality of Snackers

Tables 2 and 3 provide mean daily intake levels of dietary components for each of the age-sex groups when partitioned by the numbers of snacks consumed during 3 surveyed days. (See Analyses section for the five partitions by number of snacks. Subsequent results and discussion will also refer to these five partitions.)

Children (7 to 12 Years). For children, average daily intakes of all dietary components, except cholesterol, increased with increasing numbers of snacks consumed per day. Although not shown in Table 2, fat intake provided 40.5% of total caloric intake for the nonsnacking children, whereas 40.8%, 39.8%, 38.9%, and 37.8% of total caloric intake was obtained through fat consumption by those children who had increasing numbers

TABLE 2 Average Daily Intake of Nine Selected Dietary Components by Children (Aged 7 to 12 Years) and by Adolescent Males and Females (Aged 13 to 18 Years), Classified by Their Snack Consumption Patterns

	Dietary Components																	
	Food Energy (kcal)		Fat (g)		Cholesterol (mg)		Sodium* (mg)		Total Sugar (g)		Calcium (mg)		Vitamin B_6 (g)		Iron (mg)		Magnesium (mg)	
Number of Snacks Consumed in 3 Days	Mean	SD	Mean	SD	Mean	SD	Mean	SD	Mean	SD	Mean	SD	Mean	SD	Mean	SD	Mean	SD
Children																		
0 (N = 901)	1,690[e]†	475	76[d]	26	288[a]	152	2,215[d]	804	81[e]	33	818[c]	406	1,093[c]	428	12.1[c]	4.6	192[d]	83
1 to 3 (N = 1,677)	1,874[d]	500	85[c]	27	288[a]	144	2,443[c]	845	103[d]	38	908[b]	361	1,170[bc]	511	12.5[c]	4.9	220[cd]	184
4 to 6 (N = 1,053)	2,014[c]	524	89[b]	29	288[a]	142	2,581[bc]	888	124[c]	40	983[a]	382	1,235[ab]	543	12.8[bc]	4.7	236[c]	193
7 to 9 (N = 283)	2,173[b]	567	94[a]	32	300[a]	149	2,703[ab]	849	146[b]	52	1,023[a]	411	1,319[a]	602	13.5[ab]	5.4	271[b]	270
≥10 (N = 91)	2,287[a]	695	96[a]	36	276[a]	130	2,800[a]	1,049	164[a]	54	1,042[a]	464	1,316[a]	912	13.6[a]	6.2	318[a]	418
Adolescent males																		
0 (N = 484)	2,111[e]	688	97[d]	37	415[a]	233	2,785[d]	1,157	92[e]	44	901[d]	445	1,268[d]	582	15.1[c]	5.9	233[d]	125
1 to 3 (N = 946)	2,358[d]	726	109[c]	40	391[a]	218	3,066[c]	1,241	118[d]	46	1,041[c]	454	1,386[cd]	672	15.8[c]	6.6	281[cd]	310
4 to 6 (N = 529)	2,702[c]	793	124[b]	44	405[a]	214	3,512[b]	1,424	155[c]	60	1,280[b]	579	1,506[bc]	737	17.4[b]	7.4	318[bc]	366
7 to 9 (N = 175)	2,926[b]	811	130[ab]	44	415[a]	203	3,669[ab]	1,341	185[b]	61	1,356[ab]	626	1,563[b]	739	17.8[ab]	6.8	384[ab]	742
≥10 (N = 61)	3,116[a]	919	134[a]	44	394[a]	222	3,850[a]	1,343	206[a]	84	1,419[a]	673	1,745[a]	788	19.1[a]	6.7	397[a]	284
Adolescent females																		
0 (N = 520)	1,624[c]	554	73[c]	29	286[a]	164	2,072[c]	903	75[e]	35	706[b]	449	992[b]	482	11.5[b]	4.7	180[b]	92
1 to 3 (N = 933)	1,701[c]	538	78[c]	30	266[a]	148	2,169[bc]	886	92[d]	38	728[b]	366	954[b]	457	11.1[b]	4.7	188[b]	152
4 to 6 (N = 577)	1,891[b]	571	85[b]	32	272[a]	159	2,301[b]	901	118[c]	44	820[a]	406	1,003[b]	478	11.3[b]	4.6	205[ab]	182
7 to 9 (N = 151)	1,994[b]	557	88[b]	31	273[a]	135	2,495[a]	1,051	134[b]	48	875[a]	437	1,122[a]	833	12.8[a]	8.2	223[a]	132
≥10 (N = 59)	2,157[a]	528	97[a]	30	271[a]	147	2,552[a]	1,026	153[a]	59	893[a]	408	965[b]	446	11.8[ab]	4.0	228[a]	153

*Average sodium intake levels are underestimated because discretionary salt intake was not reported.
†Column means within each age-sex group with the same letter are not significantly different ($p \leq 0.05$).

TABLE 3 Average Daily Intake of Nine Selected Dietary Components by Adult Males and Females (Aged 24 to 44 Years) and Elderly Males and Females (65 Years and Older), Classified by Their Snack Consumption Patterns

Number of Snacks Consumed in 3 Days	Dietary Components																	
	Energy (kcal)		Fat (g)		Cholesterol (mg)		Sodium* (mg)		Total Sugar (g)		Calcium (mg)		Vitamin B_6 (g)		Iron (mg)		Magnesium (mg)	
	Mean	SD	Mean	SD	Mean	SD	Mean	SD	Mean	SD	Mean	SD	Mean	SD	Mean	SD	Mean	SD
Adult males																		
0 (N = 472)	2,056[d]†	731	101[c]	42	428[ab]	235	2,732[c]	1,247	73[d]	44	648[d]	376	1,067[b]	549	15.2[b]	6.3	220[c]	134
1 to 3 (N = 993)	2,286[c]	713	111[b]	41	446[a]	237	2,953[b]	1,268	94[c]	50	756[c]	413	1,153[a]	554	15.9[ab]	7.2	248[bc]	201
4 to 6 (N = 550)	2,448[b]	801	116[ab]	45	409[ab]	220	3,064[ab]	1,310	106[b]	55	821[b]	458	1,180[a]	573	16.1[ab]	6.0	271[b]	156
7 to 9 (N = 264)	2,597[a]	856	122[a]	50	434[ab]	234	3,189[a]	1,433	123[a]	62	887[a]	470	1,193[a]	626	16.8[a]	7.3	319[a]	295
≥10 (N = 187)	2,656[a]	898	123[a]	48	399[b]	237	3,113[ab]	1,297	127[a]	75	912[a]	452	1,177[a]	549	16.7[a]	5.9	333[a]	216
Adult females																		
0 (N = 669)	1,450[d]	495	69[c]	28	293[a]	173	1,820[c]	810	58[e]	34	479[d]	271	810[a]	383	10.8[b]	4.2	166[b]	98
1 to 3 (N = 1,317)	1,525[c]	551	73[bc]	33	287[a]	176	1,980[b]	905	69[d]	37	532[c]	319	820[a]	411	10.9[ab]	4.5	186[b]	164
4 to 6 (N = 838)	1,623[b]	520	75[ab]	30	273[a]	152	2,030[b]	861	83[c]	40	577[b]	308	845[a]	398	11.0[ab]	4.2	224[a]	317
7 to 9 (N = 373)	1,727[a]	541	79[a]	32	276[a]	167	2,155[a]	853	93[b]	45	634[a]	337	867[a]	424	11.5[a]	4.4	233[a]	226
≥10 (N = 202)	1,749[a]	601	79[a]	33	294[a]	233	2,220[a]	1,013	99[a]	56	633[a]	362	831[a]	442	11.2[ab]	4.1	240[a]	261

101

TABLE 3 Continued

Number of Snacks Consumed in 3 Days	Dietary Components																		
	Energy (kcal)		Fat (g)		Choles- terol (mg)		Sodium* (mg)		Total Sugar (g)		Calcium (mg)		Vitamin B6 (g)		Iron (mg)		Magnesium (mg)	
	Mean	SD	Mean	SD	Mean	SD	Mean	SD	Mean	SD	Mean	SD	Mean	SD	Mean	SD	Mean	SD
Elderly males																		
0 (N = 360)	1,704[c]	598	79[b]	33	382[a]	227	2,226[a]	996	72[b]	43	615[d]	320	1,087[a]	591	13.7[a]	5.6	223[a]	278
1 to 3 (N = 431)	1,900[bc]	605	89[ab]	35	389[a]	206	2,486[a]	1,025	85[b]	48	656[cd]	325	1,203[a]	656	15.0[a]	6.5	263[a]	257
4 to 6 (N = 151)	2,073[ab]	682	94[a]	42	369[a]	211	2,531[a]	898	105[a]	46	780[bc]	418	1,268[a]	691	15.3[a]	6.7	271[a]	165
7 to 9 (N = 49)	2,052[ab]	583	93[a]	33	363[a]	185	2,317[a]	894	112[a]	63	867[b]	377	1,254[a]	594	13.9[a]	5.0	296[a]	275
≥10 (N = 20)	2,160[a]	632	93[a]	35	427[a]	224	2,614[a]	968	111[a]	61	1,160[a]	814	1,285[a]	633	14.3[a]	7.0	260[a]	87
Elderly females																		
0 (N = 611)	1,352[b]	435	60[b]	23	267[a]	160	1,783[b]	727	64[d]	38	514[c]	252	939[b]	531	11.3[a]	5.2	188[b]	165
1 to 3 (N = 721)	1,414[b]	443	63[ab]	26	258[a]	154	1,830[b]	750	72[cd]	34	543[bc]	266	959[b]	469	11.1[a]	4.7	202[b]	159
4 to 6 (N = 230)	1,521[ab]	471	69[ab]	28	269[a]	156	1,877[ab]	836	82[c]	41	606[bc]	275	991[b]	496	11.4[a]	4.7	234[ab]	262
7 to 9 (N = 57)	1,681[a]	629	73[a]	41	263[a]	148	2,180[a]	1,304	102[b]	51	770[a]	435	1,223[a]	832	13.0[a]	7.3	305[a]	366
≥10 (N = 14)	1,630[a]	659	61[b]	28	223[a]	150	1,970[ab]	906	118[a]	79	643[b]	505	1,012[b]	422	13.3[a]	9.9	252[ab]	184

*Average sodium intake levels are underestimated because discretionary salt intake was not reported.
[†]Column means within each age-sex group with the same letter are not significantly different ($p \leq 0.05$).

of snacks during 3 days, respectively. Increased levels of snacking directly influenced the percentage of total caloric intake obtained from total sugar; nonsnackers obtained 19.2% of their total caloric intake from sugars, and children who consumed increasing numbers of snacks obtained 22.0%, 24.6%, 26.9%, and 28.7% for each partition, respectively. The average cholesterol intakes of all groups of children were equal to or less than the daily level of less than 300 mg recommended by the American Heart Association (1978) and the Senate Select Committee on Nutrition and Human Needs (U.S. Congress, 1977). Average sodium intakes for all groups were greater than the estimated safe and adequate (ESA) daily sodium intake of 600 mg to 1,800 mg for 7- to 10-year-olds (NRC, 1980). However, the sodium intake levels for nonsnackers and those children who consumed one to three and four to six snacks in 3 days were within the ESA levels for adolescents 11 years and older (i.e., 900-2,700 mg/day). Because these reported levels of average daily sodium intake did not include discretionary salt, these levels are of concern.

Average intake levels of the four identified problem nutrients (calcium, iron, vitamin B_6, and magnesium) indicated that although vitamin B_6 intake levels increased with increasing snack consumption, all groups had average intakes below the RDAs (NRC, 1980). For calcium, depending on the proportion of older children to younger children in the 7- to 12-year-old group, all or none of these groups of snackers met their RDA for calcium. The children that consumed snacks regularly (i.e., greater than one snack/day) most likely met their calcium needs, whereas irregular snackers probably did not. It is also more likely that the snackers consumed more appropriate amounts of iron and magnesium than did the nonsnackers.

Male Adolescents (13 to 18 Years).   For male adolescents, the average intake of dietary components for snackers versus nonsnackers followed the same patterns as those for children aged 7 to 12 years. That is, with the exception of cholesterol, there were increased levels of intake for all dietary components with increased numbers of snacks consumed. Furthermore, with increased numbers of snacks consumed, there was a decreased percentage of total caloric intake from fat (41.4%, 41.5%, 41.3%, 40.0%, and 38.7% for each partition, respectively) and an increased percentage of total caloric intake from total sugar (17.4%, 20.0%, 22.9%, 25.3%, and 26.4%, respectively). All groups of male adolescents had average cholesterol and sodium intakes in excess of the recommended levels. Vitamin B_6 average intakes were lower than the RDA for all groups, whereas average calcium intakes were lower than the RDA for only the nonsnackers and those who snacked one to three times during 3 days.

Average iron and magnesium intakes were lower than recommended for all groups except the group that snacked ten or more times in 3 days.

Female Adolescents (13 to 18 Years). Analysis of snack intake for adolescent females did not show the differences in average intakes reported for children and male adolescents. That is, with the exception of average total sugar intakes, statistically significant differences were not as pronounced. The percentage of total caloric intake from fat was similar across the groups (i.e., 40.5%, 41.3%, 40.5%, 39.7%, and 40.5% for each partition, respectively), whereas the percentage of total caloric intake from total sugar increased with increasing numbers of snacks consumed (i.e., 18.5%, 21.6%, 25.0%, 26.9%, and 28.4%, respectively). Although sodium intake increased with increasing snack consumption, the reported average sodium intakes were all within the ESA; again, however, these average intake levels did not include discretionary salt. All groups had average cholesterol intakes below the recommended 300-mg/day upper limit. Although for the most part, increases in the numbers of snacks consumed were accompanied by increased calcium, vitamin B_6, iron, and magnesium intakes, none of the groups of female adolescents had average intakes of these nutrients that were equal to their respective RDAs.

Adults (25 to 44 Years). Increased snack consumption produced increased average caloric intake for all the adult age-sex groups (Table 3). For adult males, the percentage of caloric intake from fat decreased with increasing snack consumption (44.2%, 43.7%, 42.6%, 42.3%, and 41.7% for each partition, respectively). The average cholesterol intakes all exceeded the 300-mg/day recommended level. Although average sodium intakes for each of the five groups were within the ESA range, these average intakes did not include discretionary salt. As with other age-sex groups, the percentage of total caloric intake from refined carbohydrate increased with increasing snack consumption. All the adult male groups had average iron intakes greater than the RDA. Although increased snacking resulted in increased average intakes of vitamin B_6 and magnesium, no groups had average intakes equivalent to the RDAs. Average calcium intakes were equal to or greater than the RDA for those groups of males who consumed snacks at least four to six times during 3 days, but average calcium intakes for nonsnackers and irregular snackers were less than 800 mg/day.

During a 3-day period, adult females had average fat intakes that produced from 43.1% of total caloric intake for those who had snacked one to three times to 40.7% for those who had snacked ten times or more. The average intakes of cholesterol for all groups were less than 300 mg/

day, and average sodium intakes were within the ESA level. With increased snack consumption, there was an increase in total sugar consumption as well as in the percentage of caloric intake from total sugar consumed (16.0% to 22.6%). Although in most cases increased snack consumption yielded increased intakes of all four problem nutrients, none of the partitioned groups of adult females had average intake levels of these four nutrients equivalent to their respective RDAs.

Elderly (65 Years and Older).   Average dietary component intakes for elderly nonsnackers and snackers did not vary to the extent that they did for younger age groups. For example, there were no significant differences among the snack-partitioned groups of elderly males for cholesterol, sodium, vitamin B_6, iron, and magnesium. For all groups, average cholesterol intakes were excessive, sodium intakes were within the ESA range, average iron intakes were equal to or greater than the RDA, and average vitamin B_6 and magnesium intakes were less than the respective RDAs. Although fat intakes were significantly higher for the snackers, the percentage of caloric intake from fat was highest for the men who snacked the fewest times (42.2%) and lowest for those who snacked the most times (38.8%). Percentage of caloric intake from refined carbohydrate ranged from 16.9% for nonsnackers to 21.8% for males who snacked seven to nine times during the 3 surveyed days. Only the three highest snack groups had adequate average calcium intakes.

For elderly females, the numbers of snacks consumed had no statistically significant impact on average intake levels of cholesterol or iron. These groups' average cholesterol intakes were below 300 mg/day, and their average iron intakes were adequate. Unlike all other age-sex groups, increased snack consumption was not always accompanied by a decreased percentage of caloric intake from fat (i.e., 39.9%, 40.1%, 40.8%, 39.6%, and 33.7% for each partition, respectively); however, like other age-sex groups, increased snacking was associated with an increased percentage of caloric intake from total sugar (i.e., 18.9%, 20.4%, 21.6%, 24.3%, and 29.0%, respectively). All elderly female groups had average sodium intakes (not including discretionary salt) within the ESA range. With the exception of one group, all groups of elderly females had average calcium and magnesium intakes that were less than the respective RDAs. All groups had average vitamin B_6 intakes that were less than recommended levels.

Problem Nutrients and Overconsumed Dietary Components.   Table 4 indicates the average percentages of dietary components obtained from consumed snacks for all age-sex groups. The data can be used to evaluate the extent to which snacks were responsible for increasing consumption of the problem nutrients (calcium, magnesium, vitamin B_6, and iron) and overconsumption of other dietary components (fat, cholesterol, refined carbohydrate, and sodium).

If snacks that provide a 1 to 0.66 ratio of food energy to problem nutrients are considered effective carriers of problem nutrients and those that provide the same ratio of food energy to overconsumed dietary components are designated problem carriers, then the following conclusions can be made. For all age-sex groups, snacks were effective carriers of calcium and magnesium. They were effective carriers of iron for adolescent and adult females and of vitamin B_6 for adolescent males and both elderly males and elderly females. Snacks were also problem carriers. They provided a food energy to total sugar ratio of greater than 1:0.66 for all age-sex groups, a greater than 1:0.66 ratio for sodium only for children and for male and female adolescents, and a greater than 1:0.66 ratio for fat for all age-sex groups except adult females.

In summary, these analyses showed that snacks were part of the food consumption patterns of the majority of the U.S. population. Consumed snacks provided important increases in calcium consumption, particularly among female adolescents and female adults, and in magnesium consumption for all age-sex groups. Although snacks were not identified as effective carriers of iron and vitamin B_6 among all age-sex groups, increased snack consumption was associated with increased iron and vitamin B_6 consumption. Snacks were also identified as problem carriers. They definitely increased the consumption levels of total sugar among all age-sex groups. Although grams of fat consumed generally increased with increased snack consumption, these increases were not as large as those for total sugar consumption. For most of the age-sex groups, increased snack consumption was related to decreased proportions of total caloric intake obtained from fat. Increased snack consumption was not related to increased cholesterol intake; in fact, for some age-sex groups, average cholesterol consumption was greater for nonsnackers than for snackers. Although for several of the age-sex groups average sodium intake increased with increased consumption of snacks, these increases were not dramatic, especially when considered in relation to the increased caloric consumption accompanying the increased snack consumption.

RESULTS AND DISCUSSION FOR AWAY-FROM-HOME EATING

Identification of Away-from-Home Meal Consumers

Estimated regression coefficients relating selected personal and household characteristics to numbers of meals consumed away from home during

TABLE 4 Average Proportions of Average Daily Intake of Nine Selected Dietary Components Obtained from Consumption of Snacks by Various Age-Sex Groups of Persons Classified by Their Snack Consumption Patterns

Number of Snacks Consumed in 3 Days	Dietary Components																	
	Energy (%)		Fat (%)		Cholesterol (%)		Sodium (%)		Total Sugar (%)		Calcium (%)		Vitamin B₆ (%)		Iron (%)		Magnesium (%)	
	Mean	SD	Mean	SD	Mean	SD	Mean	SD	Mean	SD	Mean	SD	Mean	SD	Mean	SD	Mean	SD
Children (7 to 12 years)																		
1 to 3 (N = 1,677)	9.4	6.4	8.4	7.7	5.2	7.2	6.2	6.4	17.2	11.4	9.0	9.0	6.3	8.8	5.3	5.9	8.8	9.3
4 to 6 (N = 1,053)	19.1	8.0	16.3	9.6	10.6	10.0	12.8	9.5	33.1	12.7	18.2	12.0	12.1	10.4	10.8	8.3	18.2	12.2
7 to 9 (N = 283)	26.7	8.9	23.0	10.9	15.3	12.8	19.0	11.8	42.3	12.5	25.1	13.6	18.2	13.0	16.4	10.0	25.7	14.2
≥10 (N = 91)	33.2	9.4	28.0	12.0	20.2	16.3	23.4	13.6	51.8	12.7	31.3	14.9	21.6	13.9	22.2	13.8	31.4	13.6
Adolescent females (13 to 18 years)																		
1 to 3 (N = 933)	10.6	7.7	8.9	8.6	6.0	8.8	7.4	8.9	20.4	14.0	9.9	10.5	6.4	8.6	5.9	6.8	9.5	9.5
4 to 6 (N = 577)	21.9	11.0	17.9	12.1	12.6	13.9	16.0	13.8	37.9	15.4	19.7	14.8	13.7	13.3	13.9	12.0	19.8	14.0
7 to 9 (N = 151)	29.5	12.4	24.4	14.4	17.5	16.1	21.6	16.4	48.3	15.1	29.5	17.4	19.4	15.7	20.3	15.6	28.5	17.5
≥10 (N = 59)	38.0	12.1	33.0	14.6	23.3	16.1	29.1	15.5	58.4	13.6	34.6	16.7	25.0	16.2	25.7	13.1	31.7	15.7
Adolescent males (13 to 18 years)																		
1 to 3 (N = 946)	10.6	8.0	9.6	9.0	6.7	9.4	8.4	9.9	18.6	12.7	10.8	11.2	7.3	9.1	7.0	8.6	10.2	11.2
4 to 6 (N = 529)	20.8	9.0	17.9	10.4	12.9	12.2	14.9	11.0	35.1	13.6	19.7	12.9	14.1	12.1	13.3	10.3	19.4	13.1
7 to 9 (N = 175)	29.1	10.0	24.6	11.6	16.2	13.0	22.0	13.3	46.9	13.9	26.7	14.4	19.3	13.3	18.5	11.9	27.0	15.0
≥10 (N = 61)	33.9	12.8	27.3	15.3	19.3	15.0	25.7	15.1	53.6	13.7	30.8	16.8	24.0	17.2	23.8	12.9	32.5	19.2

TABLE 4 · Continued

Number of Snacks Consumed in 3 Days	Dietary Components																	
	Energy (%)		Fat (%)		Cholesterol (%)		Sodium (%)		Total Sugar (%)		Calcium (%)		Vitamin B₆ (%)		Iron (%)		Magnesium (%)	
	Mean	SD	Mean	SD	Mean	SD	Mean	SD	Mean	SD	Mean	SD	Mean	SD	Mean	SD	Mean	SD
Adult males (25 to 44 years)																		
1 to 3 (N = 993)	8.9	7.4	6.4	7.4	4.3	7.3	5.7	8.2	17.5	14.4	10.0	10.9	4.6	6.5	5.1	5.9	8.2	8.3
4 to 6 (N = 550)	16.3	10.4	11.9	10.9	8.4	11.3	10.5	12.1	30.3	16.7	17.4	13.8	8.9	11.0	10.4	9.9	16.9	14.3
7 to 9 (N = 264)	21.7	11.6	15.3	12.3	9.3	10.5	12.8	12.3	38.6	18.3	22.0	15.8	11.5	12.3	13.8	10.1	22.7	14.5
≥10 (N = 187)	26.2	13.5	18.3	14.2	13.3	14.3	15.4	15.4	43.9	20.0	30.5	18.6	14.6	15.2	18.3	12.6	31.8	17.1
Adult females (25 to 44 years)																		
1 to 3 (N = 1,317)	8.7	7.4	6.7	8.0	4.7	8.7	5.8	8.4	18.7	15.3	9.6	11.3	5.2	7.6	5.5	7.0	9.0	9.8
4 to 6 (N = 838)	16.7	9.7	11.8	10.8	7.3	10.7	9.6	10.7	33.4	17.5	16.9	13.9	9.6	10.9	10.1	8.4	18.0	13.9
7 to 9 (N = 373)	22.0	10.5	15.5	11.9	9.8	11.2	12.9	12.7	43.0	17.7	22.7	15.0	13.6	12.7	15.2	9.8	25.0	14.4
≥10 (N = 202)	27.0	13.5	17.6	13.6	12.4	15.2	14.3	14.1	50.6	21.2	28.4	17.8	14.3	13.6	19.2	11.3	31.8	16.9
Elderly males (65 years and older)																		
1 to 3 (N = 431)	8.2	7.2	6.6	8.1	4.3	7.5	5.6	7.9	17.0	14.9	10.5	12.1	6.0	9.3	4.6	6.3	8.5	11.3
4 to 6 (N = 151)	16.0	8.7	12.0	9.6	8.1	11.0	10.4	10.6	28.9	15.7	19.8	15.5	11.1	11.6	9.1	7.9	15.3	11.4
7 to 9 (N = 49)	21.1	13.3	14.4	14.0	10.1	13.1	10.6	12.5	40.5	18.6	24.1	17.1	17.3	17.1	13.7	16.0	23.2	16.5
≥10 (N = 20)	25.8	11.6	16.3	16.3	10.8	11.8	14.7	13.6	34.8	18.1	30.6	18.6	18.7	19.3	16.9	9.1	26.3	16.2
Elderly females (65 years and older)																		
1 to 3 (N = 721)	8.1	6.6	6.5	7.6	4.9	9.2	5.3	7.3	17.0	14.1	10.8	11.8	6.4	9.5	5.0	7.6	8.4	10.8
4 to 6 (N = 230)	15.7	9.1	12.2	11.2	8.2	11.2	9.5	10.9	30.9	15.9	19.0	15.8	12.0	12.3	9.5	8.6	17.2	14.1
7 to 9 (N = 57)	23.2	9.8	17.7	12.2	12.8	11.9	16.6	12.2	39.3	14.9	26.0	15.6	19.0	14.0	15.5	11.6	27.8	19.3
≥10 (N = 14)	34.4	15.7	24.9	17.9	13.0	11.9	19.4	21.4	57.1	23.9	34.4	26.7	24.3	19.6	21.4	14.7	33.3	19.3

3 days surveyed for the total sample and for seven selected age-sex sub-samples are provided in Table 5. The regressions were conducted like the regressions for snacks. (See Analyses section for the five partitions by numbers of meals consumed away from home.)

Increasing per capita income had a positive effect on the numbers of meals consumed away from home by the total sample and by all age-sex groups. This effect was significant for the total sample and for four of the age-sex groups. The age-sex groups not showing a significant positive effect were children and adolescents; school lunch consumption by these persons most likely disguised the per capita income effect. The positive relationship between per capita income and numbers of meals consumed away from home is consistent with previous research (Bunch and Hall, 1983; Lippert and Love, in press; Redman, 1980; Smallwood and Blaylock, 1981). Household size did not have a strong impact on away-from-home food consumption patterns. Perhaps a relationship would have been established if a household composition variable had been incorporated in the regression analysis, as opposed to a household size variable. Both Haines (1983) and Prochaska and Schrimper (1973) found that households with children of preschool age ate away from home less frequently.

Analysis of the total sample indicated that the numbers of meals consumed away from home decreased with increasing age, a result that was probably biased because school lunch consumption patterns were included in the specification. Females consumed significantly more meals away from home than males. The significance of the time when data were collected was influenced by school lunch consumption. That is, for the total sample and for the three age-sex groups of school age, there were significantly fewer meals eaten away from home in the summer months and on weekend days. Future research in this area should make a distinction between school lunch and other kinds of meals eaten away from home.

With the exceptions of three age-sex groups, persons residing in single-headed households—either male or female—consumed more meals away from home than persons residing in dual-headed households. Haines (1983) also found that persons from single-headed households spent more for food away from home than did counterparts in dual-headed households. This result may be related to the hypothesis that a single household head who is also the primary food processor has fewer at-home labor substitutes for at-home production.

There was a strong inverse relationship between employment of a female household head and the numbers of meals consumed away from home. That is, with the exception of adult males, significantly more meals were consumed away from home when the female household head was employed. Previous studies (Kinsey, 1981; Redman, 1980) suggested that work by the female household head affected away-from-home food expenditure patterns.

With a possible exception for adolescent females, regional location of a household had little significant impact on the numbers of meals consumed away from home. The hypothesized positive relationship between degree of urbanization and numbers of meals consumed away from home was not substantiated by this analysis.

Diet Quality of Away-from-Home Meal Consumers

Guenther and Chandler (1980) reported that foods eaten away from home made positive contributions to nutrient intakes. In contrast, Cornell researchers (Bunch and Hall, 1983) found that nutrient intake was lower for those who ate some of their meals away from home. One purpose of this analysis was to test these findings.

Tables 6 and 7 provide component intake levels for each of the age-sex groups partitioned by the numbers of meals consumed away from home. For children, there were no significant differences in their cholesterol, vitamin B_6, iron, or magnesium intake levels for away-from-home food consumption patterns. All groups, except children consuming five to six meals away from home in 3 days, had cholesterol intakes less than 300 mg/day. None of the groups of children had average vitamin B_6 or magnesium intakes equal to the respective RDAs; calcium and iron intakes were consumed in more appropriate quantities. Fat, total sugar, and sodium intakes were greater for those children who consumed seven or more meals away from home. The percentage of caloric intake from dietary fat ranged from 39.8% for those who consumed five to six meals away from home to 40.5% for those who ate seven or more meals away from home. Children who consumed five to six meals away from home had the lowest percentage of calories from total sugar, whereas those who consumed seven or more meals away from home had the highest percentage.

Adolescent Males (13 to 18 Years). Regardless of the numbers of meals consumed away from home, intake levels of food energy, fat, cholesterol, sodium, vitamin B_6, and iron by adolescent males were not significantly different. Male adolescents who consumed seven or more meals away from home obtained significantly higher quantities of magnesium, whereas calcium intakes were significantly higher for those who ate three to four meals away from home. The percentage of calories obtained from fat ranged from 38.8% (seven or more meals away from home) to 41.7% (no meals away from home). The percentage of calories derived from refined carbohydrate consumption was highest for those who ate four to six meals

TABLE 5 Estimated Regression Coefficients for Per Capita Income, Household Size, Age and Sex of Person, Season of Year and Day of Week for Data Collection, and Selected Socioeconomic Variables as Related to the Number of Meals Consumed Away from Home During 3 Surveyed Days

| | | Explanatory Variables for Meals Consumed Away from Home* | | | | Season of Year | | | |
Sample†	Intercept	Per Capita Income	Household Size	Age	Sex	Summer	Fall	Winter	Weekend Days
Total (N = 18,423)	1.819‡§ (29.28)	0.051 (17.40)	-0.008 (-1.14)	-0.011 (-19.20)	0.232 (-10.57)	-0.198 (-6.68)	0.119 (4.17)	0.031 (1.08)	-0.227 (-7.36)
7–12 yrs. (N = 2,574)	1.917 (11.84)	0.018 (1.43)	-0.047 (-2.63)			-0.511 (-6.51)	0.493 (6.55)	0.421 (5.59)	-0.591 (-7.53)
13–18 yrs. male (N = 1,343)	1.382 (6.63)	0.023 (1.63)	0.004 (0.18)			0.275 (-2.54)	0.563 (5.42)	0.345 (3.40)	-0.437 (-4.16)
25–44 yrs. male (N = 1,602)	2.091 (9.91)	0.043 (5.30)	-0.047 (-1.57)			0.050 (0.44)	-0.129 (-1.15)	-0.197 (-1.85)	-2.875 (-2.87)
≥65 yrs. male (N = 523)	0.894 (3.91)	0.025 (2.82)	-0.085 (-1.88)			0.091 (0.82)	0.089 (0.85)	-0.178 (-1.67)	-0.096 (-0.87)
13–18 yrs. female (N = 1,309)	1.354 (6.05)	0.031 (1.86)	0.002 (0.09)			-0.274 (-2.56)	0.462 (4.34)	0.259 (2.36)	-0.307 (-2.82)
25–44 yrs. female (N = 2,143)	1.399 (9.40)	0.062 (7.74)	-0.065 (-3.30)			-0.130 (-1.80)	-0.095 (-1.40)	-0.222 (-3.13)	-0.128 (-1.74)
≥65 yrs. female (N = 839)	0.741 (3.92)	0.024 (3.92)	-0.127 (-3.99)			0.037 (0.50)	0.157 (2.29)	-0.045 (-0.63)	-0.115 (-1.36)

TABLE 5 Continued

Explanatory Variables for Meals Consumed Away from Home*

Sample†	Head of Household		Education		Employment		Region			Urbanization	
	Male	Female	M ≥ HS	F ≥ HS	M Not	F Not	NC	S	W	Suburban	Nonmetropolitan
Total (N = 18,423)	0.544 (8.80)	0.200 (5.80)	0.040 (1.59)	0.055 (2.22)	-0.303 (-8.16)	-0.532 (-23.89)	-0.028 (-0.94)	0.016 (0.56)	0.004 (0.12)	0.036 (1.36)	0.086 (3.17)
7–12 yrs. (N = 2,574)	0.221 (0.82)	0.166 (1.89)	0.056 (0.88)	-0.156 (-2.45)	0.123 (0.98)	-0.257 (-4.72)	-0.015 (-0.20)	0.267 (3.78)	0.108 (1.25)	0.044 (0.64)	0.219 (3.12)
13–18 yrs. male (N = 1,343)	0.715 (2.65)	0.066 (0.55)	0.038 (0.44)	0.003 (0.03)	-0.424 (-2.87)	-0.283 (-3.74)	0.242 (2.33)	0.205 (2.08)	0.274 (2.32)	0.034 (0.36)	0.150 (1.58)
25–44 yrs. male (N = 1,602)	4.263 (4.26)	-3.257 (-3.26)	1.184 (1.18)	1.055 (1.05)	-4.609 (-4.61)	-1.640 (-1.64)	-0.026 (-0.22)	-0.133 (-1.23)	-0.437 (-3.49)	-0.078 (-0.77)	-0.208 (-1.96)
≥65 yrs. male (N = 523)	0.222 (1.31)	-0.242 (-0.58)	0.154 (1.68)	0.134 (1.36)	-0.154 (-1.39)	-0.255 (-1.96)	-0.155 (-1.32)	-0.191 (-1.79)	-0.171 (-1.37)	-0.030 (-0.30)	0.163 (1.65)
13–18 yrs. female (N = 1,309)	0.064 (0.18)	0.250 (2.04)	-0.058 (-0.64)	0.077 (0.85)	-0.241 (-1.46)	-0.253 (-3.18)	0.107 (0.98)	-0.149 (-1.41)	-0.023 (-0.19)	0.361 (3.62)	0.386 (3.86)
25–44 yrs. female (N = 2,143)	3.517 (3.74)	0.432 (5.17)	-0.004 (-0.06)	0.213 (3.47)	0.050 (0.34)	-0.933 (-17.03)	-0.088 (-1.19)	0.029 (0.42)	0.041 (0.51)	0.026 (0.40)	0.012 (0.17)
≥65 yrs. female (N = 839)	-0.603 (-0.96)	0.124 (1.03)	0.162 (1.79)	0.092 (1.64)	0.057 (0.53)	-0.423 (-4.82)	-0.030 (-0.38)	0.010 (-0.14)	0.121 (1.44)	0.072 (1.05)	0.046 (0.73)

*Variables denoted as follows: M ≥ HS, male educated through high school or beyond; F ≥ HS, female educated through high school or beyond; M Not, male not employed; F Not, female not employed; NC, north central; S, South; W, West.
†Dependent variables are expressed as number of snacks consumed during 3 surveyed days.
‡Values are beta coefficients for independent variables.
§Numbers in parentheses are values of t-statistics.

TABLE 6 Average Daily Intake of Nine Selected Dietary Components by Children (Aged 7 to 12 Years) and Adolescent Males and Females (Aged 13 to 18 Years), Classified by Their Away-from-Home Meal Consumption Patterns

Number of Meals Consumed Away from Home in 3 Days	Food Energy (kcal) Mean	SD	Fat (g) Mean	SD	Choles-terol (mg) Mean	SD	Sodium* (mg) Mean	SD	Total Sugar (g) Mean	SD	Calcium (g) Mean	SD	Vitamin B$_6$ (g) Mean	SD	Iron (mg) Mean	SD	Magnesium (mg) Mean	SD
Children																		
0 (N = 1,081)	1,813[b†]	566	81[b]	30	288[a]	153	2,391[b]	938	102[b]	45	825[b]	427	1,151[a]	577	12.3[a]	5.2	214[a]	197
1 to 2 (N = 1,522)	1,894[b]	509	84[b]	27	281[a]	139	2,418[ab]	818	109[ab]	43	917[ab]	379	1,171[a]	502	12.4[a]	4.6	224[a]	172
3 to 4 (N = 1,241)	1,980[ab]	513	89[ab]	29	295[a]	141	2,551[ab]	845	112[ab]	43	1,004[a]	354	1,224[a]	516	13.0[a]	4.9	234[a]	206
5 to 6 (N = 140)	1,898[b]	505	84[b]	28	309[a]	178	2,452[ab]	885	105[b]	36	917[ab]	317	1,194[a]	424	12.7[a]	4.5	211[a]	69
≥7 (N = 21)	2,090[a]	862	94[a]	42	295[a]	165	2,685[a]	1,120	122[a]	83	842[b]	326	1,314[a]	497	12.9[a]	4.5	227[a]	68
Adolescent males																		
0 (N = 632)	2,419[a]	834	112[a]	45	417[a]	241	3,176[a]	1,306	122[a]	63	1,039[b]	530	1,400[a]	685	16.5[a]	7.0	285[b]	402
1 to 2 (N = 835)	2,404[a]	795	110[a]	43	385[a]	206	3,158[a]	1,345	129[a]	61	1,082[ab]	533	1,385[a]	742	15.9[a]	6.9	300[b]	418
3 to 4 (N = 650)	2,555[a]	754	107[a]	40	408[a]	214	3,233[a]	1,303	136[a]	57	1,198[a]	526	1,480[a]	631	16.8[a]	6.4	281[b]	165
5 to 6 (N = 61)	2,390[a]	787	107[a]	39	379[a]	209	2,956[a]	1,240	131[a]	62	1,091[ab]	509	1,232[a]	470	14.8[a]	5.6	271[b]	169
≥7 (N = 17)	2,414[a]	663	104[a]	26	456[a]	226	3,403[a]	1,230	128[a]	56	964[b]	276	1,364[a]	501	16.1[a]	6.7	472[a]	627
Adolescent females																		
0 (N = 673)	1,668[b]	619	75[b]	33	275[ab]	170	2,104[ab]	963	90[c]	46	684[b]	400	954[a]	492	11.2[a]	5.1	188[a]	157
1 to 2 (N = 847)	1,774[b]	550	81[ab]	30	279[ab]	153	2,216[ab]	900	99[bc]	44	772[ab]	428	968[a]	459	11.4[a]	4.9	195[a]	169
3 to 4 (N = 621)	1,847[ab]	527	83[ab]	29	264[ab]	135	2,337[ab]	893	108[b]	44	830[ab]	376	1,052[a]	563	11.6[a]	5.1	198[a]	112
5 to 6 (N = 81)	1,764[b]	446	80[b]	25	252[b]	147	2,071[b]	747	99[bc]	36	724[b]	363	953[a]	521	10.9[a]	3.8	187[a]	106
≥7 (N = 18)	1,983[a]	650	91[a]	34	317[a]	177	2,419[a]	972	126[a]	90	893[a]	329	1,023[a]	432	11.3[a]	3.7	225[a]	95

*Average sodium intake levels are underestimated because discretionary salt intake was not reported.
†Column means within each age-sex group with the same letter are not significantly different ($p \leq 0.05$).

away from home (21.9%) and lowest for those who consumed no meals away from home (20.2%). All groups had average cholesterol intakes in excess of the ESA range. All groups had lower than the recommended quantities of calcium, vitamin B_6, iron, and magnesium.

Adolescent Females (13 to 18 Years). Although there were no statistically significant differences in intake levels of magnesium, iron, and vitamin B_6 among the five groups of female adolescents, all groups averaged lower than the recommended quantities of these three nutrients. Average calcium intakes were less than the RDA, but were highest for those who consumed seven or more meals away from home and lowest for those who consumed no meals away from home. Average fat, cholesterol, sodium, and total sugar intakes were highest for female adolescents who consumed seven or more meals away from home and lowest for those who consumed no meals away from home. All groups had average sodium intakes that were within the ESA range. Only one group (seven or more away-from-home meals) had an excessive average cholesterol intake. The females who ate no meals away from home obtained 40.5% of their total caloric consumption from fat, whereas those who consumed increasing numbers of meals away from home obtained 41.1%, 40.4%, 40.8%, and 41.3% for each partition, respectively, of their calories from fat. Total sugar accounted for 21.6% of average caloric intake for females who consumed no meals away from home and for 22.3%, 23.4%, 22.4%, and 25.4% of average caloric intake for females who consumed increasing numbers of meals away from home, respectively.

Adult Males (25 to 44 Years). As indicated in Table 7, away-from-home meal consumption did not have a significant impact on the average consumption levels of five dietary components for adult males. Sodium intakes were highest for men who consumed no meals away from home. All five groups had average sodium intakes within the ESA range (discretionary salt not included). The percentage of total caloric intake obtained from fat ranged from 42.8% for those who consumed seven or more meals away from home to 44.2% for those who consumed five to six meals away from home. All five groups of males had average cholesterol intakes higher than the recommended maximum level. Vitamin B_6 and magnesium intakes were lower than the respective RDAs. Only the men who consumed no meals away from home had average calcium intakes equal to the RDA.

Adult Females (25 to 44 Years). Adult females who consumed five to six meals away from home had highest average intakes of fat, cho-

TABLE 7 Average Daily Intake of Nine Selected Dietary Components by Adult Males and Females (Aged 25 to 44 Years) and Elderly Males and Females (Aged 65 and Older), Classified by Their Away-from-Home Meal Consumption Patterns

Number of Meals Consumed Away from Home in 3 Days	Dietary Components																	
	Food Energy (kcal)		Fat (g)		Choles- terol (mg)		Sodium* (mg)		Total Sugar (g)		Calcium (mg)		Vitamin B$_6$ (g)		Iron (mg)		Magnesium (mg)	
	Mean	SD	Mean	SD	Mean	SD	Mean	SD	Mean	SD	Mean	SD	Mean	SD	Mean	SD	Mean	SD
Adult males																		
0 (N = 740)	2,343[a†]	871	112[a]	48	442[a]	252	3,045[a]	1,425	96[ab]	58	802[a]	488	1,202[a]	615	16.7[a]	8.2	265[a]	185
1 to 2 (N = 865)	2,302[a]	777	110[a]	43	432[a]	235	2,941[ab]	1,275	100[ab]	58	771[a]	421	1,143[ab]	608	15.6[a]	6.4	256[a]	197
3 to 4 (N = 620)	2,411[a]	745	115[a]	41	414[a]	216	3,020[a]	1,239	103[a]	56	787[a]	404	1,133[ab]	483	15.9[a]	5.4	262[a]	185
5 to 6 (N = 188)	2,241[a]	617	110[a]	39	413[a]	198	2,709[b]	1,093	90[b]	39	673[b]	343	1,045[b]	415	15.3[a]	5.6	270[a]	274
≥7 (N = 53)	2,418[a]	780	115[a]	42	459[a]	235	2,876[a]	1,175	97[ab]	50	715[ab]	402	1,035[b]	428	15.6[a]	5.2	270[a]	213
Adult females																		
0 (N = 1,593)	1,520[b]	547	70[b]	30	286[a]	117	1,963[a]	917	71[a]	42	544[a]	319	839[a]	426	11.0[a]	4.6	190[b]	166
1 to 2 (N = 1,245)	1,592[ab]	543	75[ab]	32	281[a]	171	2,002[a]	885	77[a]	41	558[a]	327	827[ab]	397	11.0[a]	4.2	208[ab]	276
3 to 4 (N = 437)	1,643[ab]	504	77[ab]	30	278[a]	162	2,044[a]	771	79[a]	40	548[a]	284	819[ab]	369	10.9[a]	3.9	209[ab]	202
5 to 6 (N = 104)	1,744[a]	546	84[a]	34	311[a]	182	2,153[a]	803	77[a]	34	554[a]	263	806[ab]	352	11.8[a]	4.8	205[ab]	127
≥7 (N = 20)	1,684[ab]	560	79[ab]	31	277[a]	141	2,097[a]	815	80[a]	39	507[a]	274	696[b]	361	10.8[a]	4.4	269[a]	369

TABLE 7 Continued

Number of Meals Consumed Away from Home in 3 Days	Dietary Components																	
	Food Energy (kcal)		Fat (g)		Cholesterol (mg)		Sodium* (mg)		Total Sugar (g)		Calcium (mg)		Vitamin B₆ (g)		Iron (mg)		Magnesium (mg)	
	Mean	SD	Mean	SD	Mean	SD	Mean	SD	Mean	SD	Mean	SD	Mean	SD	Mean	SD	Mean	SD
Elderly males																		
0 (N = 698)	1,844^a	658	86^a	38	387^a	221	2,354^a	1,012	83^a	49	676^a	371	1,150^a	632	14.4^a	6.3	250^a	278
1 to 2 (N = 234)	1,939^a	549	89^a	30	366^a	182	2,510^a	959	93^a	50	707^a	383	1,234^a	608	14.9^a	5.9	264^a	201
3 to 4 (N = 67)	1,899^a	577	89^a	36	408^a	233	2,432^a	967	88^a	44	657^a	304	1,288^a	790	14.6^a	6.6	220^a	78
5 to 6 (N = 10)	1,804^a	608	78^a	28	321^a	184	2,211^a	965	62^a	38	502^a	246	923^a	514	12.8^a	5.4	267^a	264
≥7 (N = 2)	1,597^a	314	69^a	13	293^a	273	2,489^a	57	53^a	58	646^a	375	686^a	703	12.4^a	2.3	189^a	111
Elderly females																		
0 (N = 1,131)	1,388^{ab}	458	62^{ab}	26	269^a	164	1,795^a	797	69^a	37	549^a	282	948^a	506	11.2^a	5.1	203^a	198
1 to 2 (N = 417)	1,481^{ab}	452	67^{ab}	24	247^a	131	1,921^a	733	77^a	42	548^a	268	1,003^a	538	11.8^a	5.2	210^a	182
3 to 4 (N = 74)	1,489^{ab}	503	66^{ab}	30	268^a	170	1,841^a	792	84^a	46	557^a	248	1,052^a	517	10.8^a	3.8	209^a	123
5 to 6 (N = 9)	1,667^a	461	79^a	27	253^a	103	2,378^a	1,014	70^a	38	649^a	379	766^a	299	11.5^a	2.6	222^a	79
≥7 (N = 2)	1,075^b	9.4	41^b	0.0	139^a	89	1,577^a	85	73^a	12	423^a	80	834^a	28	9.1^a	3.9	139^a	24

*Average sodium intake levels are underestimated because discretionary salt intake was not reported.
†Column means within each age-sex group with the same letter are not significantly different ($p \leq 0.05$).

lesterol, sodium, and iron and the highest percentage of caloric intake from fat consumption (43.3%). There were no significant differences among the five groups for average levels of cholesterol, sodium, total sugar, calcium, and iron intake. All groups had lower than recommended amounts of calcium, vitamin B_6, iron, and magnesium in their diets.

Elderly Males (65 Years and Older). There were no statistically significant differences among the five groups of elderly males for average intakes of the investigated dietary components. In general, average intake levels of cholesterol were more than adequate; average sodium intakes were within the ESA range; average iron intakes were adequate; and average calcium, vitamin B_6, and magnesium intakes were inadequate for all five groups. Percentages of caloric intake obtained from fat and from total sugar were lowest (38.9% and 13.5%, respectively) for the males who consumed five to six meals away from home and for those who consumed seven or more meals away from home.

Elderly Females (65 Years and Older). The only significant differences in intake levels among the five groups of elderly females were for food energy and fat; those consuming five to six meals away from home had higher intake levels than those consuming seven or more meals away from home. In general, average cholesterol intakes were appropriate, average sodium intakes were within the ESA range, and iron intakes were adequate; however, all groups of elderly females had average intakes of calcium, vitamin B_6, and magnesium that were lower than the recommended amounts.

Dietary Component Intake from Meals Consumed Away from Home. Table 8 shows the average percentages of dietary components obtained from meals consumed away from home. If it is assumed that (1) meals consumed away from home should provide a 1:1 ratio of food energy to problem nutrients and a 1:1 ratio of food energy to overconsumed dietary components and (2) errors in data collection, as well as in nutrient data banks, are such that this equivalency ratio of 1:1 can be modified by a variation of $\pm 2\%$, then the information in Table 8 can be used to evaluate persistence of differences in diet quality of away-from-home meal consumers. That is, one can observe whether, with increasing numbers of meals consumed away from home, the percentages of problem nutrients obtained from away-from-home meals were approximately equivalent (2% or less) to the percentage of food energy obtained and whether percentages of overconsumed dietary components were greater than (2% or more) percentages of food energy obtained.

For example, increased away-from-home meal consumption by children was related to increased intakes of sodium, calcium, and magnesium as well as to increased cholesterol consumption. Three or more of the reported percentages for sodium, calcium, and magnesium increased the same as the percentage of food energy, $\pm 2\%$, with increased numbers of meals consumed away from home. Two of the reported percentages for cholesterol increased the same as the percentage of food energy, $\pm 2\%$, with increased numbers of meals consumed away from home. For adolescent males, increased away-from-home meal consumption was related to increased consumption of sodium, calcium, and magnesium and somewhat related to increased consumption of cholesterol and iron. For adolescent females, there was a relationship between increased away-from-home meal consumption and proportionate increases in sodium, calcium, vitamin B_6, iron, and magnesium and a weaker association with cholesterol.

Table 8 shows that for adult males there was a strong, positive association between away-from-home meal consumption and proportionate increases in sodium, vitamin B_6, and iron intakes, whereas there was a weaker positive association with increased cholesterol intake. Results indicate a positive relationship between increased numbers of meals consumed away from home and proportionate increases in fat and iron for both adult and elderly females and in sodium for adult females. A weaker positive relationship was determined for cholesterol (in both groups of women), for sodium in elderly females, and for calcium, vitamin B_6, and magnesium in adult females. Only fat and iron showed proportionate increases in dietary component intake with increased numbers of meals consumed away from home for elderly males.

In summary, away-from-home meal consumption had somewhat different effects on diet quality for different age groups. Although increased away-from-home meal consumption by children generally provided easily observable increased intakes of food energy, fat, sodium, and total sugar, these intake patterns also provided proportionate (in relation to food energy intake) increases in cholesterol, sodium, calcium, and magnesium. For adolescent males, magnesium was the only dietary component that increased significantly with increased away-from-home meal consumption; however, proportionate increases were observed for cholesterol, sodium, calcium, iron, and magnesium. In contrast, increased away-from-home meal consumption by adolescent females resulted in increases in food energy, fat, cholesterol, sodium, calcium, vitamin B_6, iron, and magnesium. For adult males, increased away-from-home meal consumption provided significantly lower intakes of vitamin B_6 and calcium. When related

TABLE 8 Average Proportions of Average Daily Intake of Nine Selected Dietary Components Obtained from Meals Eaten Away from Home by Various Age-Sex Groups of Persons, Classified by Their Away-from-Home Meal Consumption Patterns

Number of Meals Consumed Away from Home in 3 Days	Dietary Components																	
	Food Energy (%)		Fat (%)		Cholesterol (%)		Sodium (%)		Total Sugar (%)		Calcium (%)		Vitamin B6 (%)		Iron (%)		Magnesium (%)	
	Mean	SD	Mean	SD	Mean	SD	Mean	SD	Mean	SD	Mean	SD	Mean	SD	Mean	SD	Mean	SD
Children (7 to 12 years)																		
1 to 2 (N = 1,522)	19.4	9.3	20.3	11.2	18.3	12.9	20.6	11.9	18.3	12.1	20.7	13.3	15.9	10.9	17.3	9.4	19.2	12.1
3 to 4 (N = 1,241)	38.7	10.1	40.2	12.0	37.5	16.6	41.3	12.9	37.4	14.7	42.5	14.3	33.4	14.2	34.4	12.2	39.9	13.7
5 to 6 (N = 140)	58.8	11.4	59.3	13.3	62.0	20.0	62.1	16.4	62.7	17.5	66.1	16.2	56.4	17.2	53.8	15.2	59.4	15.0
≥7 (N = 21)	74.6	14.0	73.6	15.7	80.0	16.4	76.9	15.0	73.6	17.1	74.7	16.2	77.8	17.4	77.6	14.6	75.1	19.1
Males (13 to 18 years)																		
1 to 2 (N = 835)	18.6	9.7	19.4	11.2	16.9	13.0	19.7	12.4	19.4	13.6	19.6	14.0	16.3	11.8	17.4	10.7	18.1	12.4
3 to 4 (N = 650)	36.4	11.4	37.9	13.3	33.5	17.3	38.7	14.8	34.9	15.5	38.8	15.8	31.0	14.9	32.9	13.8	35.4	14.1
5 to 6 (N = 61)	57.8	13.5	60.3	15.0	61.3	20.4	62.3	16.7	57.5	19.6	61.3	17.5	55.6	17.9	54.6	16.9	58.4	17.0
≥7 (N = 17)	83.9	13.8	85.0	14.5	89.7	15.0	86.9	12.2	80.6	17.3	85.0	14.1	85.7	14.4	86.7	11.1	86.6	11.4
Females (13 to 18 years)																		
1 to 2 (N = 847)	19.1	10.5	19.9	12.6	17.5	15.0	20.1	13.4	18.2	13.5	19.2	14.9	17.2	13.1	17.8	11.6	18.0	12.9
3 to 4 (N = 621)	38.4	12.0	39.7	14.4	36.9	18.9	40.6	15.9	37.0	16.5	40.6	18.4	33.5	16.8	35.4	14.4	37.7	15.2
5 to 6 (N = 81)	61.5	14.8	62.1	16.8	63.6	20.1	65.0	18.7	59.0	17.7	63.4	19.7	59.9	21.1	61.4	18.4	61.6	18.3
≥7 (N = 18)	79.9	17.7	82.7	17.8	84.0	16.9	83.3	16.2	73.3	23.8	81.9	19.1	82.5	19.2	83.6	16.0	80.8	21.1

TABLE 8 Continued

Number of Meals Consumed Away from Home in 3 Days	Dietary Components																	
	Food Energy (%)		Fat (%)		Cholesterol (%)		Sodium (%)		Total Sugar (%)		Calcium (%)		Vitamin B$_6$ (%)		Iron (%)		Magnesium (%)	
	Mean	SD	Mean	SD	Mean	SD	Mean	SD	Mean	SD	Mean	SD	Mean	SD	Mean	SD	Mean	SD
Males (25 to 44 years)																		
1 to 2 (N = 865)	19.0	10.6	19.7	12.6	17.5	15.4	21.0	15.0	17.2	13.9	16.8	13.0	17.2	13.2	18.6	11.8	16.1	11.6
3 to 4 (N = 620)	37.7	14.5	39.4	17.7	39.1	23.4	42.3	19.1	33.9	18.1	35.8	18.9	35.6	20.3	37.4	16.8	33.5	16.3
5 to 6 (N = 188)	58.8	18.2	60.8	21.5	63.5	24.3	62.3	19.8	54.1	20.9	55.3	21.3	58.3	22.8	58.5	20.7	56.8	20.8
≥7 (N = 53)	76.6	15.7	80.9	17.1	83.8	19.4	82.6	18.3	66.6	21.8	73.7	20.1	79.2	21.5	79.0	18.3	73.8	21.2
Females (25 to 44 years)																		
1 to 2 (N = 1,245)	19.7	11.2	20.9	13.8	18.9	17.0	20.9	15.4	16.3	13.4	16.6	13.6	18.4	15.1	18.8	12.1	16.0	12.4
3 to 4 (N = 437)	41.5	15.0	43.7	18.5	43.3	24.8	44.3	18.6	36.5	18.9	39.3	18.6	40.4	19.6	40.7	16.7	37.2	17.4
5 to 6 (N = 104)	60.0	18.1	63.6	20.6	64.5	25.0	65.4	20.5	51.2	20.4	60.6	20.9	57.7	23.5	59.9	20.2	58.5	20.9
≥7 (N = 20)	69.5	22.6	74.1	21.5	72.4	22.1	73.3	27.9	61.9	30.1	68.9	22.6	66.0	26.9	72.1	21.5	70.4	23.0
Males (65 years and older)																		
1 to 2 (N = 234)	19.5	10.4	22.0	13.4	19.4	15.6	19.0	12.5	14.4	13.6	15.5	12.1	16.8	12.7	17.6	11.1	15.7	10.3
3 to 4 (N = 67)	42.0	15.8	46.1	18.8	42.8	22.9	42.9	19.3	28.7	18.8	32.5	18.0	38.2	22.4	40.9	16.9	37.2	17.0
5 to 6 (N = 10)	62.3	14.3	73.0	18.8	70.3	22.2	68.6	13.5	46.4	25.7	49.0	20.1	58.9	28.6	63.1	20.8	48.9	20.7
≥7 (N = 2)	92.5	2.3	92.5	4.4	91.8	8.3	93.9	5.2	83.4	6.1	92.8	5.6	94.6	1.9	95.1	3.8	92.2	3.7
Females (65 years and older)																		
1 to 2 (N = 417)	21.6	11.5	24.5	14.4	22.6	17.8	19.4	13.0	15.5	14.0	15.7	12.5	18.4	14.2	19.3	11.8	17.2	11.7
3 to 4 (N = 74)	44.9	11.6	50.5	16.2	48.8	23.7	46.2	15.4	32.5	15.0	38.8	16.5	42.1	19.0	44.6	14.2	38.5	13.6
5 to 6 (N = 9)	74.1	12.0	77.8	12.8	74.6	21.0	77.1	10.9	67.4	20.9	71.7	16.3	65.9	24.9	73.5	13.0	68.2	16.7
≥7 (N = 2)	97.7	2.1	98.6	1.7	100.0	0.0	98.3	2.4	94.9	4.3	99.6	0.0	98.5	1.1	99.4	0.4	97.5	1.6

to changes in food energy intake, however, away-from-home meals provided proportionately more cholesterol, sodium, vitamin B_6, and iron. Generally, adult females who consumed increasing numbers of meals away from home had a significantly lower intake of vitamin B_6 and significantly higher intakes of fat and magnesium. For these same females, fat, cholesterol, sodium, calcium, vitamin B_6, iron, and magnesium intakes increased to a greater extent than food energy intake with increasing numbers of meals consumed away from home. Although there were no easily observable changes in dietary component intake levels with increasing numbers of meals consumed away from home by elderly males and females, proportionate increases were observed for fat and iron for both elderly males and females and for cholesterol and sodium among the elderly females.

RESULTS AND DISCUSSION FOR COMBINED ANALYSIS OF SNACKING AND EATING AWAY FROM HOME

Table 9 provides estimated regression coefficients when away-from-home meal consumption was included as an additional independent variable, influencing the percentage of calories obtained from snack consumption. Comparison of results in Table 1 with results in Table 9 shows that most of the beta coefficients remained the same in sign and significance. The important finding in Table 9 is that when the percentage of calories obtained from consumed snacks increased, away-from-home meal consumption significantly decreased.

This significant relationship between snack consumption and away-from-home meal consumption prompted the specification of two additional regressions. The total sample was partitioned into at-home meal consumers and away-from-home meal consumers. As indicated in Table 9, the persons who consumed none or very few meals away from home tended to obtain significantly more calories from snacks with increased per capita income; this relationship was not significant for persons who consumed several of their meals away from home. However, beta coefficients were the same in sign and significance for the two partitioned samples with regard to household size, age, sex, and degree of urbanization. Whereas away-from-home meal consumers obtained a significantly lower percentage of total calories from consumed snacks in the fall and winter seasons than in the spring, at-home meal consumers obtained a significantly greater percentage of total calories from consumed snacks in the summer than in the spring. In addition, the away-from-home consumers obtained more calories from snacks on weekend days; for at-home meal consumers, there was no significant difference in snack consumption for day of the week.

TABLE 9 Estimated Regression Coefficients for Personal and Household Characteristics and Number of Meals Consumed Away from Home as Related to the Proportions of Caloric Intake Obtained from Consumed Snacks for Total Sample and for Sample Partitioned into Away-from-Home Meal Consumers and at-Home Meal Consumers

Sample†	Intercept	Explanatory Variables*				Season of Year			Weekend Days	Head of Household	
		Per Capita Income	Household Size	Age	Sex	Summer	Fall	Winter		Male	Female
Total (N = 18,423)	16.000‡§ (33.97)§	0.087 (3.89)	−0.351 (−6.82)	−0.092 (−20.45)	0.249 (1.51)	0.547 (2.46)	−0.502 (−2.34)	−0.311 (−1.44)	0.413 (1.78)	0.891 (1.92)	−1.358 (−5.23)
At-home meal consumers (N = 13,868)	15.752 (29.14)	0.125 (4.44)	−0.310 (−5.28)	−0.097 (−19.16)	0.249 (1.30)	0.610 (2.42)	−0.174 (−0.70)	−0.074 (−0.30)	0.136 (0.52)	1.188 (2.03)	−1.304 (−4.35)
Away-from-home meal consumers (N = 4,555)	15.061 (16.11)	0.013 (0.36)	−0.412 (−3.81)	−0.071 (−6.58)	0.292 (0.88)	0.277 (0.58)	−1.463 (−3.46)	−1.059 (−2.46)	1.461 (2.81)	0.557 (0.70)	−1.320 (−2.53)

Table is continued on page 122.

TABLE 9 Continued

| Sample† | Explanatory Variables* | | | | | | | | | Away-from-Home Meal Consumer |
| | Education | | Employment | | Region | | | Urbanization | | |
	M ≥ HS	F ≥ HS	M Not	F Not	NC	S	W	Suburban	Nonmetropolitan	
Total (N = 18,423)	0.159 (0.83)	1.392 (7.46)	−0.224 (−0.80)	−0.330 (1.94)	−1.302 (−5.76)	−3.533 (−16.69)	−0.933 (−3.73)	1.343 (6.70)	0.188 (0.92)	−1.07 (−5.58)
At-home meal consumers (N = 13,868)	0.161 (0.73)	1.307 (6.12)	−0.021 (−0.07)	−0.130 (−0.67)	−1.506 (−5.77)	−3.651 (−14.91)	−0.831 (−2.87)	1.195 (5.17)	0.104 (0.45)	
Away-from-home meal consumers (N = 4,555)	0.121 (0.32)	1.478 (3.81)	−1.180 (−1.65)	−0.785 (−2.27)	0.620 (−1.38)	3.002 (−7.11)	−1.177 (−2.38)	1.796 (4.46)	0.522 (1.26)	

*Variables denoted as follows: M ≥ HS, male educated through high school or beyond; F ≥ HS, female educated through high school or beyond; M Not, male not employed; F Not, female not employed; NC, north central; S, South; W, West.
†Dependent variables are expressed as percentages of total caloric intake obtained from consumed snacks.
‡Values are beta coefficients for independent variables.
§Numbers in parentheses are values of t-statistics.

These results most likely indicate that the sample of away-from-home meal consumers was composed primarily of school-aged children who consumed school lunch regularly and who, during the week, had fewer hours to consume snacks. Other significant differences between snack consumption patterns for the two groups included the following: (1) Away-from-home meal consumers residing in households with only a female head ate fewer snacks than those residing in dual-headed households, whereas there were no significant differences in snack consumption for at-home meal consumers in relation to head of household. (2) Although at-home meal consumers residing in the North Central region consumed significantly fewer snacks than those residing in the Northeast, this significant difference was not present for away-from-home meal consumers.

CONCLUSIONS AND IMPLICATIONS

Snacking and eating away from home are two common food consumption patterns in the United States. Therefore, knowing who in the population exhibits these eating patterns and how these two eating patterns influence nutritional well-being is of importance to government policymakers, educators, and health-related professionals.

In general, the results of this study suggest that where and when persons eat do not strongly influence their nutritional well-being. Good nutrition requires that people learn to eat in a rational way, whether snacking, eating at home, or eating away from home. Regardless of where or when persons eat, they need to consume a variety of foods and eat them in the right proportions.

These analyses indicate possible differences in food consumption patterns of snackers versus nonsnackers and of away-from-home meal consumers versus at-home meal consumers. With our data, however, the differences are small. Thus, linking these two eating patterns to variations in persons' health status would be difficult. Perhaps future research should concentrate on population groups that are nutritionally at risk (e.g., low-income populations, less-educated populations). For the population studied here, most evidence indicated that persons consumed foods in a rational way and that where and when foods were consumed had very limited impact on their nutritional status.

REFERENCES

Abrams, I. J. 1978. Determining consumer demand and marketing opportunities for nutritional products. Food Technol. (Chicago) 32(9):79-85.

American Heart Association. 1978. American Heart Association committee report: Diet and coronary heart disease. Circulation 58:762A-765A.

Bogart, J. L., G. M. Briggs, and D. H. Calloway. 1973. Nutrition and Physical Fitness, 9th ed. W. B. Saunders and Co., Philadelphia.

Bunch, K., and L. Hall. 1983. Factors Affecting Nutrient Consumption. Agricultural Economic Research Report No. 22. Cornell University, Ithaca, N.Y.

Bundy, K. T., K. J. Morgan, and M. E. Zabik. 1982. Nutritional adequacy of snacks and sources of total sugar intake among U.S. adolescents. J. Can. Diet. Assoc. 4:358-365.

Cala, R. F., K. J. Morgan, and M. E. Zabik. 1981. The contribution of children's snacks to total dietary intakes. Home Econ. Res. J. 10:150-159.

Carroll, M. D., S. Abraham, and C. M. Dresser. 1983. Dietary Intake Source Data: United States, 1976-80. Vital and Health Statistics, series 11, no. 231. DHHS Pub. No. (PHS) 83-1681, National Center for Health Statistics. U.S. Government Printing Office, Washington, D.C.

Fischer, D. R., K. J. Morgan, and M. E. Zabik. In press. Cholesterol, saturated fatty acids, polyunsaturated fatty acids, sodium and potassium intakes of the U.S. population. J. Am. College Nutr.

Guenther, P. M., and C. A. Chandler. 1980. Nutrients in foods at home and away. Pp. 508-516 in Proceedings of the 1981 Agricultural Outlook Conference, Session #29. November 17-20, 1980. U.S. Department of Agriculture, Washington, D.C.

Haines, P. S. 1983. Away from home food consumption practices and nutrient intakes of young adults. Pp. 72-80 in Proceedings of the 29th Annual Conference of the American Council on Consumer Interests, March 16-19, 1983, Kansas City, Missouri. American Council on Consumer Interests, Columbia, Mo.

Kinsey, J. 1981. Food away from home expenditures by source of household income. Paper presented at the Annual Meeting of the American Agricultural Economics Association, Clemson, S.C.

Kornitzer, M., G. Backer, M. Dramaix, and C. Thilly. 1979. Regional differences in risk factor distributions, food habits and coronary heart disease mortality and morbidity in Belgium. Int. J. Epidemiol. 8:23-31.

Lippert, A., and D. O. Love. In press. Family expenditures for meals away from home and prepared foods—new evidence. Am. J. Agric. Econ.

McGill, H. C. 1979. The relationship of dietary cholesterol to serum cholesterol concentration and to atherosclerosis in man. Am. J. Clin. Nutr. 32:2664-2702.

McGill, H. C., and G. E. Mott. 1976. Diet and coronary heart disease. Pp. 376-391 in D. M. Hegsted, C. O. Chichester, W. J. Darby, K. W. McNutt, R. M. Stalvey, and E. H. Stotz, eds. Present Knowledge in Nutrition, 4th ed. The Nutrition Foundation, Inc., New York.

Morgan, K. J., and M. E. Zabik. 1983. Michigan State University Nutrient Data Bank, 4th ed. Michigan State University, E. Lansing.

NRC (National Research Council). 1980. Recommended Dietary Allowances, 9th ed. A report of the Food and Nutrition Board, Assembly of Life Sciences. National Academy of Sciences, Washington, D.C.

Pao, E. M., and S. J. Mickle. 1980. Nutrients from meals and snacks. Pp. 495-507 in Proceedings of the 1981 Agricultural Outlook Conference, Session #29. November 17-20, 1980. U.S. Department of Agriculture, Washington, D.C.

Pooling Project Research Group. 1978. Relationship of blood pressure, serum cholesterol, smoking habit, relative weight and ECG abnormalities to incidence of major coronary events: Final report of the pooling project. J. Chronic Dis. 31:201-306.

Prochaska, F., and R. Schrimper. 1973. Opportunity cost of time and other socioeconomic effects on away from home food consumption. Am. J. Agric. Econ. 53:597-603.

Putnam, J. J., and M. G. Van Dress. 1984. Changes ahead for eating out. Nat. Food Rev. 26:15-17.

Redman, B. J. 1980. The impacts of women's time allocation on expenditures for meals away from home and prepared foods. Am. J. Agric. Econ. 62:234-237.

Shekelle, R. B., A. M. Shryrock, O. Paul, M. Lepper, J. Stamler, S. Liu, and W. J. Raynor. 1981. Diet, serum cholesterol and death from coronary heart disease. The Western Electric study. N. Engl. J. Med. 304:65-70.

Smallwood, D., and J. Blaylock. 1981. Impact of Household Size and Income on Food Spending Patterns. Technical Bulletin No. 1650, National Economics Division, Economics and Statistics Service. U.S. Department of Agriculture, Washington, D.C.

SASI (Statistical Analysis System Institute). 1982. SAS User's Guide. Sparks Press, Raleigh, N.C.

U.S. Congress. 1977. Dietary Goals for the United States, 2nd ed. Senate Select Committee on Nutrition and Human Needs, U.S. Senate, 95th Congress, 1st Session, December 1977. U.S. Government Printing Office, Washington, D.C.

USDA (U.S. Department of Agriculture). 1980. Food and Nutrition Intakes of Individuals in 1 Day in the United States. Spring 1977. Nationwide Food Consumption Survey 1977-78. Preliminary Report No. 2. U.S. Department of Agriculture, Hyattsville, Md.

USDA (U.S. Department of Agriculture). 1984. Nutrient Intakes: Individuals in 48 States, Year 1977-78. Nationwide Food Consumption Survey, 1977-78. Report No. I-2. U.S. Department of Agriculture, Hyattsville, Md.

USDA and USDHEW (U.S. Department of Agriculture and U.S. Department of Health, Education, and Welfare). 1980. Nutrition and Your Health: Dietary Guidelines for Americans. U.S. Government Printing Office, Washington, D.C. 15 pp.

Variety in Foods

HELEN SMICIKLAS-WRIGHT, SUSAN M. KREBS-SMITH,
and JAMES KREBS-SMITH

Nutritionists generally accept the idea that eating a variety of foods ensures the selection of a nutritionally adequate diet. In the United States, variety is a fundamental tenet of dietary guidance, representing the first of seven guidelines issued by the U.S. Department of Agriculture and the U.S. Department of Health and Human Services (USDA and DHHS, 1980). Furthermore, Recommended Dietary Allowances (RDAs) issued by the Food and Nutrition Board of the National Research Council are "intended to be met by a diet of a wide variety of foods rather than by supplementation or by extensive fortification of single foods" (NRC, 1980, p. 1). Indeed, from the 1920s to the present, the idea of variety has continued, although changes have occurred in the suggested kinds and amounts of food to eat (Wolf and Peterkin, 1984).

The notion that a variety of food choices enhances the likelihood of selecting a nutritionally adequate diet is not limited to food guidance in the United States. Canada's *Food Guide* recommends variety in food choices and eating patterns as a basic nutrition principle (Department of National Health and Welfare, 1979). Food variety is also recommended for people in developing countries, such as rural populations with limited-food patterns (Robson and Wadsworth, 1977).

This paper addresses two questions: (1) What is food variety? (2) What benefits does an increasingly varied diet provide? Pertinent literature is reviewed, and some preliminary data are presented on variety in American diets and the relationship between variety and dietary quality.

REVIEW OF LITERATURE

Food variety has been described as a simple guideline, but one that represents a complex food selection technique (Wolf and Peterkin, 1984). The complexity is illustrated by the diversity and proliferation of food products on supermarket shelves. The average supermarket may contain 15,000 items (Connor, 1980), and thousands of new products are introduced each year (Solomon, 1983). Although many new products may be no more than minor alterations in flavor or package size, the general picture is one of immense choice.

This vast selection of food items may be responsible for consumers' difficulty in understanding the concept of variety. A Canadian study (Department of National Health and Welfare, 1979) examined consumer understanding of such nutrition concepts as adequate diet, balanced diet, and food variety. When asked to interpret the advice, "Eat a variety of foods each day," many respondents simply listed different kinds of foods. Some stated that it meant eating different kinds of meat or balanced meals. About one-third of respondents reported that variety meant a little of everything, and about 15% described it as not eating the same food every day.

Consumer confusion about variety may arise not only from the plentitude of food products but also from the professional community's various interpretations of, and recommendations for, variety. One interpretation of variety is that it represents the selection of foods from among major food groups. For example, *Nutrition and Your Health: Dietary Guidelines for Americans* advises consumers to include selections from six food groups: fruits; vegetables; whole grain and enriched breads, cereals, and grain products; milk, cheese, and yogurt; meats, poultry, fish, and eggs; and legumes (USDA and DHHS, 1980).

A second interpretation of variety is the selection of foods from within food groups. *Ideas for Better Eating: Menus and Recipes to Make Use of the Dietary Guidelines* recommends choosing different foods within each group of foods and emphasizes more servings of fruits, vegetables, and grain products—especially whole grains—and frequent consumption of dark-green vegetables, dry bean dishes, and starchy vegetables (USDA, 1981).

In a third interpretation of variety, Canada's *Food Guide* recommends varying food preparation methods—for example, using raw, cooked, canned, and frozen fruits and vegetables (Department of National Health and Welfare, 1982). It suggests that even more variety may be achieved by altering the size of meals and the time and location in which meals are eaten.

Perhaps the various interpretations stem from the many expected benefits of food variety. Probably the most frequently stated benefit is the increased assurance of adequate nutrient intakes (Guthrie, 1977). Other benefits from variety include avoiding either deficiencies or excesses of single nutrients (USDA and DHHS, 1980), ensuring an appropriate balance of micronutrients (Mertz, 1984), and reducing the likelihood of exposure to contaminants in any single food item (USDA and DHHS, 1980). Variety has also been recommended as a way of increasing eating enjoyment (Department of National Health and Welfare, 1979). Few of these specific benefits of variety have been closely examined, although several researchers have studied the importance of food variety in general (Black and Sanjur, 1980; Caliendo *et al.*, 1977; deGwynn and Sanjur, 1974; Duyff *et al.*, 1975; Krondl *et al.*, 1982).

Krondl and coworkers (1982) measured food variety in the diets of elderly Canadians by asking how many of 181 commonly available foods were eaten in the previous year. Participants were classified as having diets of limited variety or greater variety. The mean, less one standard deviation, was selected as the cutoff point separating limited from greater variety. Thus, 49 or fewer items represented limited variety, and 50 or more represented greater variety. Variety of food use was determined for 90.8% of sampled women and 69.4% of sampled men. Greater variety was associated with higher educational achievement, higher health rating, and a stronger effort to maintain health. However, the study did not measure nutrient intakes, which would have allowed comparisons between variety and nutritional adequacy.

Sanjur and coworkers used food diversity scores to study dietary patterns in various populations (Black and Sanjur, 1980; Caliendo *et al.*, 1977; deGwynn and Sanjur, 1974; Duyff *et al.*, 1975). Duyff and coworkers (1975) examined the diets of Puerto Rican-American teenagers by measuring food diversity and nutritional adequacy. Diversity was defined as the average number of different food items eaten by a respondent per day. Intakes of calcium, iron, vitamin A, and vitamin C were calculated from a 3-day record. The mean diversity per day—12.5 items—was described as low. More diverse diets were reported to be more nutritionally adequate; however, the data on this relationship were not presented.

Another study examined food diversity among Puerto Rican women attending a maternal and infant care clinic (Black and Sanjur, 1980). The diversity score was constructed as follows. From a frequency distribution of all food items consumed in a 24-hour period, the 16 food items most frequently consumed were selected. Women who consumed fewer than 8 of the selected items received a score of 1; women who consumed from 8 to 11 selected items received a score of 2; and women who consumed more than 11 of them received a score of 3. Results showed that women who were migrants to the community had higher diversity, nutrition knowledge, and food preference scores. Nutritional adequacy was not measured in the study.

Yet another food diversity score was computed by Caliendo and co-workers (1977) in their study of 113 preschool children residing in New York State. The score was based on the number of foods consumed by 20% or more of the children during a 24-hour period; the reported number was 20.

Absent from the literature is information on the extent to which American diets exhibit variety and how variety improves the quality of those diets. Such information could provide a more precise interpretation of variety for consumers. To meet this need, we measured variety in various sex and age groups and examined the relationships of dietary variety to both nutritional adequacy and macronutrient balance.

METHODS

Study Population

Data for this study were obtained from the basic survey portion of USDA's 1977-1978 Nationwide Food Consumption Survey (NFCS) (USDA, 1980). In that survey, individual household members recalled 1 day's food intake and kept a diary for 2 additional days. Information was gathered from a stratified area probability sample of 15,000 households in the 48 conterminous states and the District of Columbia (USDA, 1980). Determining which persons in each household would be asked to participate differed by season. In the spring, all persons in each household were asked to provide food intake information. In the fall, winter, and summer, only one-half of those persons 19 years of age and older were asked to participate, except for those persons in one-member households who were asked to participate regardless of age. Proportional representation was maintained in these other seasons by double counting each record for respondents 19 years of age and older, except for respondents from one-member households. Additional weighting factors were applied to all persons in the survey to account for nonrespondent households. Three-day food records were obtained from 28,030 persons (36,255 weighted). In order to save costly computer time, only a subsample of that population was analyzed in the present study.

The NFCS sample population used for this study was selected as follows. From the unweighted spring portion of the NFCS, a straight 10% random sample was selected. For the other seasons, in order to achieve an appropriate age distribution, a 10% random sample of all persons 19 years or older, regardless of household size, was selected. After the sample was drawn, pregnant and lactating females and children under 1 year of age were excluded. Although the study population was not a representative sample of the U.S. population, it represented a large group of people more than 1 year of age from all regions of the United States.

Variety Measure

Variety was defined as the number of unique food items, characterized by distinct NFCS code numbers, that were consumed and reported in 3 days. Such a scoring system is simple yet accounts for as much variation as possible within the NFCS data. The individual food codes differentiated items on the basis of such factors as added ingredients, preparation method, and extent of fat removal. Table 1 presents some examples of NFCS food codes and their descriptions.

Overcounting and undercounting of unique food items are possible with the NFCS food codes. For example, some identical foods, variously described, have different codes. If a person reported the same food in different ways, overcounting of unique food items would occur, and results would erroneously show more variety in food consumption. Similarly, some NFCS food codes refer to food mixtures (e.g., sandwiches, casseroles). If one person reported eating a tuna salad sandwich and another person, consuming the same food, reported eating bread, tuna, mayonnaise, and celery, undercounting of unique food items would occur for the former person, and results would erroneously show less variety in food consumption.

Overcounting, however, was determined to have a negligible effect on results, and adjustment for undercounting could not be made because

TABLE 1   1977–1978 Nationwide Food Consumption Survey Examples of Food Codes[a]

Food Code	Description
111–1100	Milk, cow's, fluid, whole
111–0000	Milk, not further specified
111–1211	Milk, cow's, fluid, low fat (2%)
115–1100	Milk, chocolate
581–0503	Macaroni and cheese
581–0519	Cheese ravioli, no sauce
581–2113	Rice casserole, no cheese

[a]From USDA, 1980.

(1) the NFCS code book does not include all ingredients of mixtures and (2) counting ingredients could invalidate a mixture as a unique food item if the ingredients were also reported elsewhere as individual food items.

Because a simple measure of variety was desired for this study and because correction for all overcounting and undercounting was impossible, the study proceeded with the number of unique food codes on each person's record as the measure of variety; this measure was labeled unique foods.

Dietary Quality Measures

Dietary quality was assessed by two measures of nutrient adequacy (nutrient adequacy ratios and mean adequacy ratios) and by the percentage of calories from fat, protein, and carbohydrate. Nutrient adequacy ratios (NARs) were calculated for 10 nutrients (protein, calcium, iron, magnesium, phosphorus, vitamin A, thiamin, riboflavin, vitamin B_{12}, and vitamin C) according to the following equation:

$$NAR = \frac{\text{person's 3-day average intake of nutrient}}{\text{RDA of nutrient}}.$$

A second NAR was calculated for vitamin B_6, but the value listed in the RDA table (NRC, 1980) was not used as the denominator. Instead, we used 0.02 mg of vitamin B_6 per gram of protein intake. Vitamin B_6 values in the RDA table were based on this formula but were also based on an assumption that many adults consume an average of 100 g to 110 g of protein. Many adults, however, do not consume such high levels of protein; therefore, the RDA table values may overestimate the need for vitamin B_6 (Guthrie and Crocetti, 1983).

A mean adequacy ratio for 11 nutrients (MAR11) was calculated by adding the percent RDAs met (truncated at 100%) for each of 11 nutrients and dividing the sum by 11. Therefore, an MAR11 of 100 represents 100% of the RDAs for all nutrients included in the score.

RESULTS

Extent of Variety

The number of unique foods reported by this study population varied from 4 to 63 (Table 2), and all age and sex groups showed a wide range of unique food consumption. Children as young as 1 to 3 years of age displayed variety, ranging from 12 to 45 different items. The mean number

TABLE 2   Mean Number and Range for Unique Food Items and for
Total Number of Foods Reported in 3 Days by Sex and Age of
Respondents

Sex	Age (years)	Number of Persons	Number of Unique Foods		Total Number of Foods	
			Mean ± SD	Range	Mean ± SD	Range
Male	1–3	82	24.9 ± 7.0	12–43	40.9 ± 11.1	19–70
	4–6	86	27.1 ± 6.5	7–44	41.5 ± 9.8	20–64
	7–10	136	28.1 ± 6.7	15–46	41.7 ± 9.2	23–70
	11–14	135	27.8 ± 7.2	6–49	43.2 ± 12.3	17–79
	15–18	157	27.4 ± 7.1	10–46	42.4 ± 12.4	15–76
	19–22	115	24.6 ± 7.8	9–46	38.3 ± 11.4	16–67
	23–50	566	27.5 ± 7.9	4–56	45.0 ± 14.6	9–109
	51–69	269	27.1 ± 8.3	7–56	48.1 ± 16.5	8–112
	≥70	117	25.7 ± 7.9	4–50	50.1 ± 14.4	12–93
Female	1–3	69	24.1 ± 6.3	12–45	39.5 ± 9.4	24–70
	4–6	93	26.2 ± 6.0	8–40	40.4 ± 8.5	22–64
	7–10	124	28.5 ± 7.2	11–48	42.4 ± 9.9	20–70
	11–14	137	27.4 ± 7.1	5–47	40.0 ± 10.3	7–66
	15–18	138	24.2 ± 7.5	7–50	36.7 ± 12.0	9–76
	19–22	118	23.7 ± 8.2	7–51	35.9 ± 12.2	12–71
	23–50	751	25.3 ± 8.1	4–63	40.4 ± 13.9	7–119
	51–69	405	26.6 ± 8.2	6–61	45.5 ± 13.6	9–98
	≥70	203	24.2 ± 6.8	9–50	44.2 ± 12.1	16–93
Total		3,701	26.2 ± 7.8	4–63	42.7 ± 13.5	7–119

of unique foods for the total sample of 3,701 persons was 26.2 ± 7.8.
The mean number of unique foods for each age and sex group was similar—approximately 25 foods.

The number of total food items reported (total foods), also shown in
Table 2, ranged from 7 to 119. As with unique foods, all age and sex
groups exhibited wide ranges. However, there are some sex and age
differences in the mean values for total foods reported. Males aged 23
years and older had the highest mean values; females aged 15 to 22 years
had the lowest mean value.

To simplify reporting of the results, the population was divided into
seven groups based on the number of unique foods reported (1-15, 16-
20, 21-25, 26-30, 31-35, 36-40, and 41 or more) and eight groups based
on total foods reported (1-10, 11-20, 21-30, 31-40, 41-50, 51-60, 61-70,
and 71 or more) (Tables 3-7).

Table 3 displays, for the total group, the mean number of unique foods
and total foods and the percentage of persons in each unique foods and
total foods category. Relatively few persons, 7.3% of the total sample,

TABLE 3 Mean Number of Unique Foods and Total Foods Reported by Sample Population and Percentage Distribution of Persons Who Reported Consuming Various Numbers of Unique Foods and Total Foods in 3 Days (N = 3,701)

Measure	Mean ± SD	Number of Foods	Percentage of Persons Reporting
Unique foods	26.2 ± 7.8	1–15	7.3
		16–20	16.2
		21–25	24.4
		26–30	24.6
		31–35	15.8
		36–40	7.4
		≥41	4.3
Total foods	42.7 ± 13.5	1–10	0.3
		11–20	3.0
		21–30	14.5
		31–40	29.4
		41–50	27.2
		51–60	15.9
		61–70	6.8
		≥71	2.9

consumed fewer than 16 unique foods, and an even smaller number, 4.3%, consumed 41 or more unique foods. The mean total foods score was about 43, most persons reporting between 20 and 60 total food items.

Relationship Between Variety and Various Quality Measures

Table 4 presents the bivariate relationships between unique foods and each of the 11 NARs. All the NARs showed a positive relationship with the measure of variety used here. Variation in the number of unique foods appeared to account for more variation in the magnesium and thiamin NARs than in other nutrient NARs. In contrast, relatively little NAR variation for protein, iron, and vitamins B_6 and B_{12} was explained by variations in unique foods. Except for the lowest unique foods category, the NARs for protein were high.

Table 5 presents the distribution of persons in each unique foods category by MAR11 score. With each increase in number of unique foods, the proportion of persons with MAR11 scores of less than 60 dropped precipitously, whereas the percentage of persons with scores of 80 or higher multiplied several times. Less than 1% of those with 20 or fewer unique foods achieved an MAR11 score of 100, and almost none with more than 30 unique foods had a score of less than 60.

TABLE 4 Mean Nutrient Adequacy Ratios (NARs), by Number of Unique Foods Reported in 3 Days, and Correlation Coefficients

Nutrient	Mean NARs by Number of Unique Foods							Correlation Coefficient (r)[b]
	1–15 (N = 270[a])	16–20 (N = 601)	21–25 (N = 905)	26–30 (N = 910)	31–35 (N = 584)	36–40 (N = 273)	≥41 (N = 158)	
Protein	0.85[c]	0.95	0.98	0.99	1.00	1.00	1.00	0.33
Calcium	0.52	0.63	0.71	0.77	0.83	0.88	0.89	0.38
Iron	0.62	0.72	0.80	0.85	0.88	0.91	0.92	0.34
Magnesium	0.53	0.64	0.73	0.80	0.85	0.90	0.91	0.49
Phosphorus	0.78	0.88	0.94	0.97	0.98	0.99	0.99	0.38
Vitamin A	0.57	0.68	0.77	0.84	0.89	0.92	0.95	0.39
Thiamin	0.64	0.80	0.88	0.92	0.95	0.97	0.98	0.44
Riboflavin	0.71	0.84	0.91	0.95	0.97	0.98	0.98	0.41
Vitamin B_6	0.84	0.85	0.86	0.88	0.89	0.90	0.91	0.15
Vitamin B_{12}	0.71	0.83	0.90	0.92	0.95	0.97	0.97	0.33
Vitamin C	0.55	0.71	0.81	0.88	0.93	0.95	0.98	0.41

[a]Number of persons reporting.
[b]Correlation of unique foods and NAR. All correlations are significant at $p \leq 0.0001$.
[c]NARs are truncated at 1.00.

TABLE 5 Percentage Distribution of Mean Adequacy Ratios for 11 Nutrients (MAR11) Obtained from Various Numbers of Unique Foods in 3 Days

Number of Unique Foods Reported	N^a	Distribution of MAR11 Scores (%)				
		Scores <40.0	Scores 40–59.9	Scores 60–79.9	Scores 80–99.9	Scores >100
1–15	270	9.3[b]	26.3	37.4	26.7	0.4
16–20	601	1.5	11.3	38.8	47.4	1.0
21–25	905	0.1	3.9	24.5	70.3	1.2
26–30	910	0.0	0.4	16.4	79.1	4.1
31–35	584	0.0	0.2	17.2	87.5	5.1
36–40	273	0.0	0.0	4.0	86.5	9.5
≥41	158	0.0	0.0	2.5	81.0	16.5
Total	3,701					

[a]Number of persons reporting.
[b]Percentages may not total 100 due to rounding.

Table 6 shows the mean percentage of caloric intake from protein, fat, and carbohydrate for each unique foods category. As the number of reported unique foods increased, there was a slight decrease in mean percentage of caloric intake from protein and a corresponding increase in mean percentage of caloric intake from carbohydrate. Interestingly, the mean percentage of caloric intake from fat was virtually the same for all unique food categories. Another study (Guthrie and Wright, 1984) in which a different subset of the NFCS population was used showed that as unique foods increased, the percentage of reported meats and meat alternatives decreased slightly, whereas reported fruits and vegetables increased.

TABLE 6 Mean Percentage of Caloric Intake Obtained from Protein, Fat, and Carbohydrate by Persons Who Reported Consuming Various Numbers of Unique Foods in 3 Days

Number of Unique Foods Reported	N^a	Caloric Intake		
		From Protein (%), Mean ± SD	From Fat (%), Mean ± SD	From Carbohydrate (%), Mean ± SD
1–15	270	18.4 ± 5.1	39.1 ± 9.8	41.7 ± 12.5
16–20	601	16.9 ± 3.5	40.2 ± 7.8	42.5 ± 10.1
21–25	905	16.9 ± 3.2	40.5 ± 7.1	42.3 ± 8.9
26–30	910	16.2 ± 3.2	40.8 ± 6.6	42.8 ± 8.3
31–35	584	16.0 ± 2.8	40.5 ± 6.4	43.6 ± 8.3
36–40	273	15.5 ± 2.8	40.6 ± 5.8	43.9 ± 7.8
≥41	158	15.4 ± 2.5	40.9 ± 5.2	43.7 ± 6.9
Total	3,701			

[a]Number of persons reporting.

TABLE 7   Mean Number of Kilocalories Obtained per Day by Males and Females (Aged 23 to 50 Years) Who Reported Various Numbers of Unique Foods in 3 Days (N = 1,317)

Number of Unique Foods Reported	Males		Females	
	N^a	kcal, Mean ± SD	N	kcal, Mean ± SD
1–15	36	1,719 ± 500	80	858 ± 357
16–20	68	2,069 ± 634	134	1,234 ± 392
21–25	136	2,158 ± 568	185	1,464 ± 424
26–30	133	2,407 ± 608	179	1,704 ± 495
31–35	107	2,684 ± 773	98	1,853 ± 371
36–40	56	2,806 ± 651	41	1,940 ± 430
≥41	30	2,880 ± 611	34	2,199 ± 665
Total	566		751	

^{a}Number of persons reporting.

The relationship between the mean number of kilocalories (kcal) obtained per day and the number of unique foods reported was also examined in this study. Table 7 shows values for males and females aged 23 to 50 years. For both sexes, mean caloric values increased as unique foods increased. For males who reported the least variety, the mean daily caloric intake was 1,719 kcal; for those males who reported 41 or more different items, mean daily caloric intake was 2,880 kcal. Women who reported 1 to 15 items had a mean caloric intake of 858 kcal, whereas those who reported 41 or more foods obtained 2,199 kcal. All age and sex groups showed similar relationships.

Because there seemed to be no reason that variety per se would increase caloric intake to such an extent, another question emerged. Perhaps variety, as defined by the unique foods measured here, was interrelated with the absolute number of foods eaten (total foods). If the unique foods measure was highly correlated with total foods, this might explain the positive relationship between variety and caloric intake. Indeed, the correlation between unique foods and total foods for this population was determined to be 0.76. In other words, 58% of the variation in unique foods is explained by total food scores.

This interrelationship prompted the reexamination of the relationship between unique foods and MAR11—this time controlling for total foods reported. The relationship was examined by a correlation-regression analysis, using MAR11 as the dependent variable and unique foods, total foods, and the interaction of unique and total foods as independent variables. Table 8 shows the equation obtained by regression analysis. This can be used as a model to predict MAR11. There is a significant interaction between unique foods and total foods in their relationship

TABLE 8   Equation Obtained by Regression Analysis to Predict MAR11 Score by Number of Unique Foods and Total Foods Reported in 3 Days[a]

Parameter	Regression Coefficient (b value)
Number of unique foods	1.68[b]
Total number of foods	0.95[b]
Interaction	−0.02[b]
Intercept	28.07

[a]MAR11 = 28.07 + 1.68 (unique foods) + 0.95 (total foods) [b] − 0.02 (unique foods × total foods).
[b]$p \leq 0.0001$.

to MAR11 scores. This interaction suggests that the effect of variety on overall nutritional adequacy is different for various numbers of foods eaten.

Table 9 shows the estimated MAR11 scores that can be predicted from the model for various numbers of total foods and unique foods. Although these are not actual sample means, these data fit the model reasonably well. Regardless of the total number of foods reported, MAR11 scores increased with increasing variety, but the amount of change associated with an increase in unique foods was greater when total foods were low than when total foods were high. Therefore, when only 20 foods were reported in 3 days for every 1 unit increase in unique foods, a 1.3 unit increase in MAR11 scores was expected. However, when 60 food items were eaten in 3 days, only about a 0.5 unit increase in MAR11 for such an increase in unique foods was expected.

TABLE 9   Estimated Mean Adequacy Ratios for 11 Nutrients (MAR11s), by Total Number of Foods and Various Numbers of Unique Foods Reported in 3 Days

Number of Unique Foods Reported	Estimated MAR11s				
	20 Total Foods	30 Total Foods	40 Total Foods	50 Total Foods	60 Total Foods
15	66.3	72.8	79.3	85.8	92.3
20	72.7	78.2	83.7	89.2	94.7
25		83.6	88.1	92.6	97.1
30		89.0	92.5	96.0	99.5
35			96.9	99.4	101.9[a]

[a]MAR11s are truncated at 100, but the linear relationship suggests that at high levels of both unique foods and total foods, average untruncated MAR11s would exceed 100.

SUMMARY AND DISCUSSION

The goal of nutrition education is to provide simple and reliable advice to consumers that will guide them in selecting a healthful diet. Such a diet must not only provide adequate amounts of the essential nutrients but also must guard against excessive consumption of kilocalories and harmful constituents.

Although the advice to "eat a variety of foods" sounds like a simple axiom, consumers may be confused about implementing the recommendation. Even within the nutrition community, there are various interpretations of how variety is to be achieved. Nutritionists expect many benefits from variety, although few of these benefits have been tested.

This study examined the extent of variety in American diets and the effect of variety on dietary quality. A variety measure was selected to account for as much total variation in food choice as possible—including variation among and within major food groups and variation from altered cooking methods. Use of this simplified measure to examine bivariate relationships initially suggested that increased variety was associated with improved nutritional adequacy. This result seemed to confirm one major stated purpose of food variety—the selection of a nutritionally adequate diet.

However, further analysis determined that variety was also related to the total number of foods that a person ate. In this study population, persons with increased variety consumed more foods. The accompanying high NARs and caloric intakes may have resulted more from increased total foods than from increased variety. Therefore, nutritionists must be cognizant of their implicit advice to increase the number of foods when they suggest eating a variety of foods.

Furthermore, when the number of foods was controlled and variety examined, earlier conclusions about the relationship between variety and overall nutritional adequacy (MAR11) required alteration. That is, variety affected overall nutritional adequacy less when the number of foods was high and more when the number of foods was low. This suggests that dietary variety is more important for persons consuming a limited number of foods, such as females aged 15 to 22 years.

Further research on food variety is necessary so that nutritionists can provide the best dietary guidance to consumers. Our ongoing research examines the relationships between variety (controlling for the total number of foods) and the other measures of dietary quality—the individual NARs, caloric intake, and percentage of caloric intake from each of the macronutrients. We are also studying the separate effects of dietary variety within and among major food groups, e.g., whether food variety within some groups is more important to dietary quality than in other groups, or how dietary quality is affected when a person simply chooses foods by food group without regard to choices within groups. This research needs to be accompanied by studies that identify how consumers interpret variety when they are faced with a complex food supply. Such research will contribute significantly to dietary guidance.

ACKNOWLEDGMENT

This research was partially supported by Contract 58-3198-2-57 from the Human Nutrition Information Service, Consumer Nutrition Center, U.S. Department of Agriculture.

REFERENCES

Black, S. J., and D. Sanjur. 1980. Nutrition in Rio Piedras: A study of internal migration and maternal diets. Ecol. Food Nutr. 10:25-33.

Caliendo, M. A., D. Sanjur, J. Wright, and G. Cummings. 1977. Nutritional status of preschool children: An ecological analysis. J. Am. Diet. Assoc. 71:20-26.

Connor, J. 1980. Food product proliferation: Part II. Natl. Food Rev. Summer:10-13.

deGwynn, R. E., and D. Sanjur. 1974. Nutritional anthropometry, diet and health-related correlates among preschool children in Bogota, Colombia. Ecol. Food Nutr. 3:273-281.

Department of National Health and Welfare. 1979. Nutrition Concepts Evaluation Study. Nutrition Education Unit, Health Promotion Directorate, Health Services and Promotion Branch, Ottawa, Ontario, Canada.

Department of National Health and Welfare. 1982. Canada's Food Guide: Handbook. The Ministry of Health and Welfare, Health Promotion Directorate, Ottawa, Ontario, Canada.

Duyff, R. L., D. Sanjur, and H. Y. Nelson. 1975. Food behavior and related factors of Puerto Rican-American teenagers. J. Nutr. Educ. 7:99-103.

Guthrie, H. A. 1977. Concept of a nutritious food. J. Am. Diet. Assoc. 71:14-19.

Guthrie, H. A., and A. F. Crocetti. 1983. Implications of a protein-based standard for vitamin B_6. Nutr. Rep. Int. 28:133-138.

Guthrie, H. A., and H. S. Wright. 1984. Assessing Dietary Intake. Second Report for Contract 58-3198-2-57. The Human Nutrition Information Service, Consumer Nutrition Center, U.S. Department of Agriculture, Washington, D.C.

Krondl, M., D. Law, M. A. Yurkin, and P. H. Coleman. 1982. Food use and perceived food meanings of the elderly. J. Am. Diet. Assoc. 80:523-529.

Mertz, W. 1984. The essential elements: Nutritional aspects. Nutr. Today 19:22-30.

NRC (National Research Council). 1980. Recommended Dietary Allowances, 9th ed. A report of the Food and Nutrition Board, Assembly of Life Sciences. National Academy of Sciences, Washington, D.C.

Robson, J. R. K., and G. R. Wadsworth. 1977. The health and nutritional status of primitive populations. Ecol. Food Nutr. 6:187-202.

Solomon, G. 1983. New foods proliferate without high technology. Nutr. Week 13(26):4-6.

USDA (U.S. Department of Agriculture). 1980. Food and Nutrient Intakes of Individuals in One Day in the United States, Spring, 1977. Nationwide Food Consumption Survey 1977-78, Preliminary Report No. 2. U.S. Department of Agriculture, Washington, D.C.

USDA (U.S. Department of Agriculture). 1981. Ideas for Better Eating: Menus and Recipes to Make Use of the Dietary Guidelines. U.S. Government Printing Office, Washington, D.C.

USDA and DHHS (U.S. Department of Agriculture and U.S. Department of Health and Human Services). 1980. Nutrition and Your Health: Dietary Guidelines for Americans. HG232. U.S. Government Printing Office, Washington, D.C. 20 pp.

Wolf, J. D., and B. B. Peterkin. 1984. Dietary guidelines: The USDA perspective. Food Technol. 38:80-86.

IV
Perspectives on Nutrition Programs, Policy, and Research

Introduction

JEAN-PIERRE HABICHT

The following papers represent viewpoints from some institutions and elements of American life that influence nutrition policy, programs, and research: the scientific community, the food industry, the U.S. Department of Agriculture, the legal sector, and educators. The authors' ideas are quite conventional when compared to the new approaches to nutrition presented in Session 2, "What Factors Shape Eating Patterns?" Perhaps when traditional nutrition approaches (biochemical and clinical) are coupled with insights from psychology, economics, and sociology about the determinants of nutrition, answers to improving nutrition in the U.S. population will be found.

The Role of Nutrition Research in Policy and Program Planning

JEAN-PIERRE HABICHT

Perceived needs motivate policies and programs. As these are implemented, additional perceptions about needs result in new and changed policies and programs. Scientific research can improve this process by helping to define needs and by encouraging the development of effective, efficient, and equitable policies and programs to meet them.

Nutritionists measure nutrient needs according to the National Research Council's Recommended Daily Allowances (RDAs) and Recommended Energy Intakes (REIs) (NRC, 1980). These measures are used to estimate inadequate intakes in populations. However, those scientists who set the RDAs and REIs gave insufficient consideration to the potential harm of safety margins that are too generous, and nutritionists who use the RDAs to interpret intake data from population surveys pay insufficient heed to the safety margins, which are variously inflated for various nutrients. Reported results, then, may show erroneously high inadequate intakes of some nutrients and distorted ranking of nutrients of public health concern. The Research Council's Food and Nutrition Board, which is responsible for setting the RDAs, is examining this use of the RDAs for assessing the prevalence of nutritional problems (NRC, in press).

Another issue that needs scientific attention is whether nutritional problems affect a few persons or many, which would determine the policies and programs that are required. Clinical occurrences are not necessarily public health concerns amenable to public health and other nonclinical interventions that are appropriate only when a significant portion of a population is affected. Of course, consideration is given not merely to the number of persons afflicted but also to where those persons are clustered either geographically or within particular groups. The identification of such clusters depends on adequate nutrition surveillance.

At the level of the total population, the United States is in the forefront in developing nutritional monitoring mechanisms. These systems, in which large national probability samples are surveyed, demonstrate that nutritional deficiencies in the United States today are relatively uncommon. (See paper by Woteki and colleagues in the first section of this volume.) In those rare instances in which classical nutritional deficiencies are identified, they affect low numbers of the general population. Some high-risk groups, however, are simply not picked up by our current surveillance system: the elderly, the homeless, runaway children, migrant laborers, and vagrant, psychologically debilitated persons. In short, all those without a residence or who do not respond to voluntary surveys are not sampled by current surveillance systems.

To provide these unsampled persons with a safety net that goes beyond simply providing food, they must be identified, their nutritional needs understood, and appropriate strategies developed to meet their needs. Present surveillance systems are inadequate for this purpose. Large national probability samples, an essential component of any national nutrition surveillance system, will not reveal prevalent nutritional problems—even if such problems are clustered. Nor will local probability sample surveys do much better. Therefore, a new, different kind of mechanism that can ascertain the needs of the few who are physiologically undernourished must be developed.

Although there are few persons who suffer observable ill effects from malnutrition, many persons do not eat well, according to what Americans consider to be a suitable diet (Physician Task Force on Hunger in America, 1985). For Americans, a minimum suitable diet, in contrast to a physiologically adequate one, not only prevents overt malnutrition but also is psychologically and culturally acceptable, even if it is more expensive than a physiologically adequate but less acceptable diet. This attitude is, in fact, embodied in the policy underlying the U.S. Department of Agriculture's thrifty food plan (Code of Federal Regulations, 1982). It is therefore inappropriate to use only measures of physiological adequacy to determine whether persons have enough to eat. Nutritionists must redefine suitable diet, based on physiology, economics, and food likes and preferences.

The classical nutritional deficiencies and unsuitable diets that typically concern nutritionists are not responsible for the nutrition-related illnesses that affect most Americans. For example, the major nutrition-related cause of death among teenagers and young adults in the United States today is alcoholism. Although the solutions to alcoholism may be unfamiliar to nutritionists, the problem needs their concern and research. Another example: dental caries is a nutritionally caused health problem with the highest incidence in the United States, although it is not a classic life-threatening deficiency disease. And, in contrast to what many people believe, the most feasible approach to preventing dental caries is not simply to curtail sugar intake but to increase food resistance by the use of fluoride (Horowitz, 1980). Furthermore, the feasibility of increasing fluoride intake by means of water and salt fluoridation is proven and under way, whereas no intervention that decreases sugar intake has been shown to be feasible on a large scale. Nutritionists could help decrease the incidence of dental caries by more forcefully supporting these findings in public education and policy formulation.

Most deaths and disabilities in the United States are caused by yet other diseases in which nutrition has either an etiologic, contributory, or exacerbating influence: atherosclerosis, stroke, diabetes, cancer, and osteoporosis. For these diseases, knowledge about the nutritional contribution is less well defined, and effective preventive interventions by nutritionists and others are still tentative.

In spite of incomplete knowledge about nutrition and chronic diseases, enough is known or strongly suspected so that a prudent and informed person will select a diet different from the typical American diet. Such a diet, however, may not fulfill the RDAs (NRC, 1980). For example, lowering of recommended total fat and salt intakes for disease prevention is almost incompatible with American palates and pocketbooks if the diet must also fulfill all the RDAs. If one also wants to consume a diet with fewer potential carcinogens and more protective factors against cancer, attaining the RDAs is jeopardized even more. One solution to this problem is for scientists to add these considerations to the physiological ones of the past when they set guidelines for a healthy diet. These considerations include concern for persons who wish to choose their own diets wisely, for dietetic counseling, for institutional food procurement, for food and nutrition policy, and for nutritional surveillance. Such an action requires an authoritative group, such as the Research Council's Food and Nutrition Board (which, in fact, now envisages this initiative), to look beyond the biochemical and clinical aspects of nutrition and to incorporate findings from epidemiology, economics, psychology, and other sciences in these new recommendations.

REFERENCES

Code of Federal Regulations. 1982. Section 271. Title 7, Agriculture; Chapter II, Food and Nutrition Service; Subchapter C, Food Stamp and Food Distribution Program; Part 271, General Information and Definitions. Office of the Federal Register, Washington, D.C.

Horowitz, H. S. 1980. Theme 1—The prevention of oral disease. Established methods of prevention. Br. Dent. J. 149:311–318.

NRC (National Research Council). 1980. Recommended Dietary Allowances, 9th ed. A report of the Food and Nutrition Board, Assembly of Life Sciences. National Academy of Sciences, Washington, D.C.

NRC (National Research Council). In press. Nutrient Adequacy: Assessment Using Food Consumption Surveys. A report of a committee of the Food and Nutrition Board, Commission on Life Sciences. National Academy Press, Washington, D.C.

Physician Task Force on Hunger in America. 1985. Hunger in America. The Growing Epidemic. Harvard University School of Public Health, Boston, Mass. 147 pp.

The Food Industry and Nutrition

GILBERT A. LEVEILLE

Investigations of eating patterns and nutritional adequacy often seem to be based on the following two assumptions: (1) that food selection is and has been the major determinant of nutritional status and (2) that any change in eating behavior will negatively affect nutritional status. I would like to take issue with these assumptions and assert that the food industry has had a strong positive impact on the improvement of the food supply and, hence, on nutritional status. This influence provocatively suggests the only way to improve diets. If future changes in diet composition can be agreed on, they will be affected primarily by changing the food supply rather than food selection behavior. How can these changes best be implemented?

A cooperative effort among academia, government, and the private sector is essential for dealing with present and future nutrition issues, and scientific consensus is critical to that effort. Because recommendations for action are difficult to implement unless there is scientific support, scientific consensus is the essential element for creating workable public policy that will rally the private sector to creatively change the food supply and thereby achieve the identified objectives. An example is illustrative.

Nutrition research and subsequent cooperative efforts among academia, government, and the food industry resulted in the virtual eradication of deficiency diseases (Heybach et al., in press). No longer do hundreds of thousands of Americans die of pellagra each year, nor do we see children with bowed legs resulting from rickets. Goiter, a result of iodine deficiency, is not commonplace, as it once was in many parts of the United

States. The elimination of nutrient deficiency disease was not the result of better food selection (i.e., consumers simply following the recommendations of nutrition researchers). Rather, it was the result of the food industry modifying the food supply—of adding iodine to salt, vitamin D to milk, and enriching cereal. Information from nutrition research led to a consensus on nutritional benefits and, eventually, to policies that the food industry could and did implement.

The contemporary nutritional issues that demand the kind of cooperative effort described above are more complex than those of the past. Inadequate nutrient intake is still a concern. And although calcium, magnesium, iron, zinc, pyridoxine, and folic acid intakes fall short of desirable levels, caloric intake appears to be excessive for many Americans (Pao and Mickle, 1981). Achieving lower caloric intakes with the existing food supply would further lower nutrient intake. The objective—to ingest more nutrients and fewer calories—requires a more nutrient-dense diet. Such a diet can be achieved by careful consumer selection of foods, an effective but unlikely solution. A better solution would be the evolution of a more nutrient-dense food supply.

Another contemporary and complex nutrition issue involves the view that better health can result from particular diets, for example, diets lower in fat, particularly saturated fat; lower in cholesterol; lower in calories; lower in salt; higher in fiber. Most consumers would have difficulty selecting and maintaining these diets. The food industry, however, could make a contribution

• if nutritional goals were clearly defined and supported by scientific consensus;

• if consumers were sufficiently convinced to purchase new products; and

• if manufacturers differentiated between the new, improved and the old products in their marketing.

The essential element for this process to occur is a clear scientific mandate for changes in our food supply. It can lead to workable public policy and regulations that in turn provide the framework for an effective food industry response.

REFERENCES

Heybach, J. P., G. D. Coccodrilli, and G. A. Leveille. In press. The contribution of processed food intake to the nutrient status of the U.S. population. In R. S. Harris and E. Karmas, eds. Nutritional Evaluation of Food Processing, 4th ed. AVI Publishing Co., Inc., Westport, Conn.

Pao, E., and S. J. Mickle. 1981. Problem nutrients in the United States. Food Technol. 35:58-79.

Nutrition Education

JOHANNA T. DWYER

Many factors, including economics, personal lifestyles, trends in the food supply, and psychology, exert powerful influences on what people eat. Consumers do not base food choices largely on their consideration of the right mix of nutrients for optimal health and disease prevention. However, many consumers want and will use health-related nutritional advice that takes all the reasons they eat into account and phrases dietary recommendations in ordinary language at the level of food choice (Dwyer, 1984). The task for nutrition scientists is to develop such recommendations, especially for those most likely to be at nutritional risk; to test their utility; and to communicate them to appropriate target groups.

Three misconceptions related to nutrition education research and policy limit our ability to make sound recommendations:

- Scientists know what the most nutritionally vulnerable are eating today.
- The basic four food guide (described later in this chapter) is the best food guide for the 1980s.
- Diets of the general population are unrelated to diets prescribed for medical or therapeutic purposes.

Nutrition scientists can help to dispel these misconceptions by recognizing the realities that refute them and making appropriate recommendations for action.

EATING PATTERNS OF THE NUTRITIONALLY VULNERABLE

Misconception 1: Scientists know what the most nutritionally vulnerable are eating today. In reality, little is known about the current dietary intakes of some nutritionally vulnerable subgroups, especially those who are multiply vulnerable because of several risk characteristics.

Swann (1983) has recently reviewed evidence on dietary intakes of the population obtained from the U.S. Department of Agriculture (USDA) Nationwide Food Consumption Survey (NFCS) and the U.S. Department of Health and Human Services (DHHS) Health and Nutrition Examination Surveys (HANES). These surveys provide benchmark data about what the population ate at the time the surveys were conducted. They also provide some helpful nutrition information on subgroups within the population, such as the poor. However, these surveys have two limitations. First, because they survey a representative sample of the entire population, it is not possible to sample all the subgroups that may be of particular interest, that is, those that possess a constellation of risk factors believed to confer nutritional vulnerability. Such subgroups include the poor who are ill or who have physical or mental disabilities, the poor who have recently migrated to this country from war-torn countries in Southeast Asia or countries in the Western Hemisphere, illegal migrants, and the mentally ill who are homeless. Current estimates of how many of these persons are under- or malnourished differ considerably.

A second limitation of these surveys is that they are dated; results are several years old, and times have changed. Obtaining timely nutritional information is important, especially for high-risk groups, when, for example, changes in social welfare and public assistance programs, especially those involving categorical grants, are being contemplated. Since federal grants of the categorical type are for very specific purposes, such as nutrition, arguments in favor of continuing or discontinuing them should be based in part on the evidence of their effects on nutritional status.

Recommendations

Several recommendations emerge from this picture of the nutritionally vulnerable. First, existing surveillance efforts should continue. Since 1980, the budget of the National Center for Health Statistics has been cut by 28%, and staff reductions have totaled 12% (Burnham, 1984). Further cuts in major programs for descriptive statistics on the food consumption and health of the population must be avoided in both USDA and DHHS. It is vital that the federal government continue to collect these descriptive statistics. It is unlikely that surveys conducted by private or voluntary groups could ever be sufficiently large to provide valid samples of the entire population. Nor would statistics derived from such surveys be regarded as authoritative and plausible by all the various parties and interest groups that are involved in making national nutrition policy. Regardless of what the federal government's role is in health and nutrition intervention programs, the government clearly is responsible for documenting food consumption and health status of the population and characteristics of groups that are especially likely to be adversely affected by nutrition policy. These kinds of data are particularly important if states, localities, and nongovernmental groups will, in the future, assume greater responsibility for social intervention programs.

A second recommendation is that nutrition-monitoring mechanisms must be developed. These mechanisms could be integrated with the existing nutritional status surveillance systems to increase timeliness, improve coordination, and increase target group specificity (e.g., focus on groups that are expected to experience particular nutritional problems).

A third recommendation is that groups at high nutritional risk should be assessed for the potential effects that any changes in government programs might have. These groups include the so-called "attractive" vulnerable people, such as pregnant women, infants, and children, as well as the "unattractive" vulnerable people—whose problems are even more profound—such as the homeless, the mentally ill, the indigent sick, and refugees. With data available now, it is possible to guess how changes in categorical programs would be likely to affect these groups; if several categorical grant programs were cut simultaneously, the effects would be even more pronounced. With present data, however, it is impossible to make predictions about their ultimate effect on nutritional status.

When assessing effects of government program changes on groups at high nutritional risk, it is important to evaluate more carefully persons who have several characteristics that impart nutritional risk, such as poverty—or near poverty—combined with poor health, poor education, or other disabilities. Many of the legislative changes in the Omnibus Budget Reconciliation Act of 1981 (P.L. 97-35) were crafted without these careful evaluations. This led to sometimes needless disruption and suffering among a number of disadvantaged groups (Nathan and Doolittle, 1983; Palmer and Sawhill, 1984). One example is the confusion wrought by this law among many disabled and deserving Social Security insurance disability recipients whose payments were terminated and then restored after a considerable delay. The end result was few or no monetary savings and great anxiety among this vulnerable population.

Federal and state executive agencies also need to be judicious, compassionate, and aware of how simultaneous changes in several categorical grants (such as Elderly Meals) and entitlement programs (such as Medicare and Social Security) may affect vulnerable populations. It is their responsibility to write regulations that minimize negative effects on these groups. In addition, the academic community, especially community nutrition researchers, must improve its documentation of the natural history of changes in dietary status and nutritional health of various groups at high nutritional risk as programs change. In spite of major changes in the economy and in categorical programs in recent years (Nathan and Doolittle, 1983; Palmer and Sawhill, 1984), few solid studies reporting the effects of program changes on health and nutritional status have appeared in peer-reviewed journals. These descriptive studies have potential impact on policy and thus are too important to leave to social welfare advocates or their critics to conduct with the use of indirect measurements of nutritional and health effects.

FOOD GUIDANCE SYSTEMS

Misconception 2: *The basic four food guide was the best food guide in the 1950s, and it remains so today.* The guide recommended specified numbers of servings to be eaten each day from four food groups: fruits and vegetables; meat, poultry, fish, eggs, and beans; breads, grains, and cereals; and milk and milk products. In reality, other, better food guidance systems exist for the 1980s. The so-called "basic five" guide, which adds fats, sweets, and alcohol, is a step in the right direction but not quite far enough.

There is ample evidence that Americans are not presently obtaining enough of some key nutrients (Pao and Mickle, 1981). And a recent publication demonstrated that the basic four food guide does not adequately assist American consumers in the 1980s with good eating habits (Crocetti and Guthrie,1983). It is well known that the Recommended Dietary Allowances in their present form (NRC, 1980) and the *Dietary Guidelines for Americans* (USDA and DHHS, 1980) also have limitations for planning family meals or as eating guides (Dwyer, 1981).

The principles embodied in the basic four guide, that is, sufficiency, variety, and balance, are still valid. However, food guidance must also address economic issues, moderation, the enormous variety of available foods, current eating habits, and diet-related problems. Several guides that deal with these issues are available. *Nutrition and Your Health: Dietary Guidelines for Americans* (USDA and DHHS, 1980) was the first attempt to modify the basic four guide by stating some additional principles about nutrient intake and suggesting their applications. Also helpful is a recently released food guidance system that was developed by the USDA for the American Red Cross's nutrition course (American National Red Cross, 1984). It includes a good food guide as well as additional nutrition education materials for age and physiological groups with special needs. Another good food guide is USDA's *Ideas for Better Eating* (USDA, 1981). Several new publications on diet for consumers may also be available soon from DHHS.

The development of a single food guidance system that all public, private, and voluntary groups endorse is probably impossible. However, it may be possible to develop consensus statements on general nutrition principles that could be included in all systems. The National Institutes of Health (NIH) Consensus Conferences on various biomedical issues may offer the forum to develop these statements. For example, one of the NIH Consensus Conferences in 1985 was devoted to obesity and its health risks; conferences on other issues that must be resolved for the development of food guidance materials should also be held. These conferences have the benefit of being more specific and perhaps more removed from partisan politics and the policymaking process than are such committees as the executive branch's Dietary Guidelines Review Committee. At the very least, such consensus conferences and other forums can supplement and enrich the other policymaking committees. They can be used as a basis for developing special recommendations for specific therapeutic purposes.

Recommendations

Observations of past and present food guidance systems suggest that the most recent ones, for example, the basic four and basic five food guides and USDA's *Ideas for Better Eating* (1981), should be evaluated with consumer testing. The empirical results of such testing should then be examined and the systems changed accordingly so that nutritional advice fits the dietary actualities of Americans in the 1980s and takes into account public understanding of the scientific issues involved (Funkhauser, 1972).

Nutrition education materials should be developed for nutritionally vulnerable, high-risk groups (e.g., refugees and illegal migrants from Latin America, Haiti, and Southeast Asia). They should be based on the best food guidance systems and results from studies of the groups' characteristics and lifestyles. These materials should be useful adjuncts to food, health, and other assistance programs. Because these persons' lives differ from those of the mainstream population with respect to economic levels, education, health status, and in some cases, culture, special efforts will be needed. Federal involvement is essential because private and local government resources and expertise do not exist to develop such materials.

PREVENTIVE AND THERAPEUTIC DIETS

Misconception 3: Nutritional recommendations for persons at risk for, or who already suffer from, a particular disease are unrelated to recommendations for the general population. In reality, the eating patterns, food supply, and diets of the larger society exert important influences on those persons who eat modified diets for preventive or therapeutic reasons. Moreover, therapeutic recommendations are based on usual recommendations in most respects. The larger nutritional environment can be supportive or destructive to the maintenance of special dietary regimens, such as low-fat, low-protein, or low-calorie diets.

Recent research findings suggest a role for diet in the treatment of disease. Some examples include the possible role of low-protein therapeutic diets in delaying chronic renal failure and hemodialysis (Alvestrand *et al.*, 1982; Barsotti *et al.*, 1981; Maschio *et al.*, 1982; Mitch, 1984); the need for reexamining the recommended restriction of simple carbohydrates and emphasis on complex carbohydrates in diabetic diets (Jenkins *et al.*, 1982; Kolata, 1983); and the possible role of low-fat diets in preventing colon and breast cancers (Hernandez, 1984).

Investigators are testing such hypotheses with metabolic studies in humans (Hernandez, 1984; Mitch, 1984), and NIH has recently launched two feasibility studies for large-scale clinical trials involving high-risk patients or patients who are already suffering from cancer of the breast or early end-stage renal disease. The ease with which patients adhere to special diets in these trials will vary, depending on how the food supply and food habits change. For example, if low-fat products become more widely available to consumers, patients in the lipid-lowering and breast cancer trials will find it easier to eat diets very low in fat without making extraordinary efforts to do so. In addition, with regard to experimental design, dietary changes in the larger population may alter the number of subjects needed to detect true differences between those on usual diets and those on experimental diets, if such differences do exist.

Recommendations

One recommendation regarding nutritionally vulnerable people is that descriptive research is needed on the diets and diet-related beliefs of persons who are at risk for a disease or who have been prescribed diets for chronic degenerative diseases requiring therapeutic dietary alterations. What these persons actually believe or do about diet is not well known (Dwyer, 1983; McNutt, 1980). It is important to describe the eating habits of these persons in order to develop nutrition education efforts to help them.

A second recommendation is to develop authoritative guidelines to clarify for the public the differences between preventively oriented diets for those at risk of disease and therapeutic diets for those already afflicted by disease. Consumers are often unaware of the differences, and without consulting their physicians, they may mistakenly embark on extremely modified diets of their own devising. The elderly and those at high risk for cancer are groups especially likely to do so.

CONCLUSIONS

Federal support for biomedical research, including nutrition research, has been relatively strong over the past decade (Dickson, 1984). Advances in fundamental knowledge have been considerable, and it is important that such support continue. Modest support for nutrition education research is needed, as are funds for maintaining and expanding descriptive research—based on nutritional and health statistics—that will better monitor nutritionally vulnerable high-risk groups. These applied research efforts should result in nutrition policy that is more sound and in the application of nutrition science to the daily lives of Americans.

REFERENCES

Alvestrand, A., M. Ahlberg, P. Furst, and J. Bergstrom. 1982. Clinical results of long-term treatment with a low protein diet and a new amino acid preparation in patients with chronic uremia. Clin. Nephrol. 19:67-73.

American National Red Cross. 1984. Better Eating for Better Health. American National Red Cross, Washington, D.C.

Barsotti, G., A. Guidicci, F. Ciardella, and S. Giovanetti. 1981. Effects on renal function of a low nitrogen diet supplemented with essential amino acids and ketoanalogues and of hemodialysis and free protein supply in patients with chronic renal failure. Nephron 27:113-117.

Burnham, D. 1984. Staff cuts for statistical agencies are studied. New York Times, Friday, November 23, p. A24.

Crocetti, A. F., and H. A. Guthrie. 1983. Eating Behavior and Associated Nutrient Quality of Diets. Anarem Systems Research Corporation, New York.

Dickson, D. 1984. Pp. 11-56 in the New Politics of Science. Pantheon Books, New York.

Dwyer, J. T. 1981. Consumer needs for the translation of the recommended dietary allowances. Pp. 237-257 in the Beltsville Agricultural Research Symposium Proceedings. U.S. Department of Agriculture, Washington, D.C.

Dwyer, J. T. 1983. Dietary recommendations and policy implications: The U.S. experience. Pp. 315-355 in J. Weininger and G. Briggs, eds. Nutrition Update, Vol. 1. John Wiley and Sons, New York.

Dwyer, J. T. 1984. The optimal diet: An impossible dream? National Forum (Phi Kappa Phi) Winter:10-14.

Funkhauser, G. R. 1972. Public understanding of science: The data we have. Presented at the Workshop on the Goals and Methods of Assessing the Public's Understanding of Science. Materials Research Laboratory, Pennsylvania State University, University Park, Pa.

Hernandez, T. B. 1984. Fat and Breast Cancer: Summary of Literature Review of Epidemiologic and Metabolic Studies in Humans. JWL International Corporation, Annandale, Va.

Jenkins, D. J. A., R. H. Taylor, and T. M. S. Wolever. 1982. The diabetic diet, dietary carbohydrate and differences in digestibility. Diabetologia 23:477.

Kolata, G. 1983. Dietary dogma disproved. Science 220:487-488.

Maschio, G., L. Oldrizzi, and N. Tessitore. 1982. Effects of dietary protein and phosphorus restriction on the progression of early renal failure. Kidney Int. 22:371-376.

McNutt, K. 1980. Dietary advice to the public. Nutr. Rev. 19:570-578.

Mitch, W. E. 1984. The influence of the diet on the progression of renal insufficiency. Annu. Rev. Med. 35:249-264.

Nathan, D., and E. Doolittle. 1983. The Consequences of Cuts. Princeton University Press, Princeton, N.J.

NRC (National Research Council). 1980. Recommended Dietary Allowances, 9th ed. A Report of the Food and Nutrition Board, Assembly of Life Sciences. National Academy of Sciences, Washington, D.C.

Palmer, J., and I. Sawhill. 1984. The Reagan Record. Urban Institute, Washington, D.C.

Pao, E. M., and S. J. Mickle. 1981. Problem nutrients in the United States. Food Technol. 35:69-79.

Swann, P. S. 1983. Food consumption by individuals in the United States: Two major surveys. Annu. Rev. Nutr. 3:413-432.

USDA (U.S. Department of Agriculture). 1981. Ideas for Better Eating: Menus and Recipes to Make Use of the Dietary Guidelines. U.S. Government Printing Office, Washington, D.C.

USDA and DHHS (U.S. Department of Agriculture and U.S. Department of Health and Human Services). 1980. Nutrition and Your Health: Dietary Guidelines for Americans. HG232. U.S. Government Printing Office, Washington, D.C. 20 pp.

Assessment of Diet Quality and the U.S. Department of Agriculture's Nutrition Policy and Research

BETTY B. PETERKIN

Several facts about diets in the United States are basic to nutrition policy, research, and programs:

- The American food supply is plentiful and varied.
- Most Americans have enough to eat—some too much.
- Diets of Americans differ widely.
- Factors affecting American diets are numerous—many of them unknown or not quantified.
- What, when, and where Americans eat change over time.
- Many Americans might benefit from dietary modification. Precisely what modifications will produce specific benefits await further research.

POLICY

The food and nutrition policy of the U.S. Department of Agriculture has the following mission: to ensure that all Americans have access to (1) an adequate, safe, and nutritious diet and (2) the information needed to make informed food choices (Block, 1983; USDA, 1984). The department carries out its nutrition mission through research, information, education, regulations, and food assistance programs.

158

RESEARCH

To help Americans improve their diets, continued research on what and why Americans eat is necessary (Peterkin and Rizek, 1984). USDA's new Continuing Survey of Food Intakes by Individuals initiated in early 1985 will provide continuous data on diets of a core group of the population (Rizek and Posati, 1985). By means of a major decennial survey planned for 1987, the USDA will obtain information on household food use and costs and 3-day intakes of household members. Several studies (Peterkin and Rizek, 1984), some just completed and others planned, have been designed to improve the reliability of dietary data and speed up the reporting process.

Translation of food intake data to nutrient intake data requires reliable information on food composition. Considerable research progress has been made in recent years, both in the development of methods for nutrient analysis and the availability of nutrient data on increasing numbers of foods. Because of these advances, diets reported in the 1985 survey can be assessed for almost twice the number of nutrients as were used in the 1977-1978 national survey (USDA, 1980).

The success of the USDA food and nutrition mission depends on researchers' ability to define diets that promote optimum health and prevent disease. The definition of such diets is complicated by researchers' uncertainties about human nutritional requirements, about availability and interaction of nutrients in the body, and about the relationship of diets to the prevention of disease. Even if those concepts were understood, nutrition education approaches to translate this understanding into improved eating behavior would be needed.

PROGRAMS

Nutrition and Your Health: Dietary Guidelines for Americans, published jointly by the USDA and the U.S. Department of Health and Human Services (USDA and DHHS, 1980), presents current dietary guidance policy; these guidelines are the basis for nutrition education programs and for the nutritional standards of the food assistance programs. The seven dietary guidelines are now under review by the Dietary Guidelines Advisory Committee (Wolf and Peterkin, 1984). Historically, USDA has interpreted "Eat a variety of foods," currently guideline no. 1, to mean that people should eat foods that together provide the Recommended Dietary Allowances (RDAs) (NRC, 1980). USDA has identified the RDAs—defined by the National Research Council as "adequate to meet the known nutritional needs of practically all healthy persons"—as the appropriate standard for guidance. Few Americans, especially American women, consume diets that meet RDAs for all nutrients (Pao and Mickle, 1981), and U.S. food supplies are not sufficient to provide the population with RDAs of some nutrients (Welsh and Marston, 1982). Furthermore, to achieve RDAs while meeting guideline no. 2, "Maintain ideal weight," requires extreme dietary change for some sex-age categories (Cleveland *et al.*, 1983).

Thus, even without considering the other five guidelines relating to fat, cholesterol, sugar, sodium, alcohol, carbohydrate, and fiber, there is a major nutrition program dilemma. Should USDA's nutrition education and food assistance program objectives call for the major disruption of food consumption patterns necessary to achieve RDAs for nutrients—especially nutrients for which no apparent public health problem exists? We do not know the risk associated with failing to achieve RDAs. Perhaps the RDA committee was unduly cautious in establishing RDAs where nutrient requirements are uncertain. Nutrition educators and food program planners must be aware of this uncertainty if they are to help the public make wise food choices. If the RDAs are not appropriate standards for dietary guidance and food programs, such standards must be developed.

Eating patterns of Americans differ widely and are always changing in response to a myriad of factors. One factor that concerns many nutritionists is dietary guidance itself, and several questions need continuing research.

- Are the nutrition guidelines that are prepared for the public by the federal government, the nutrition community, health professionals, self-proclaimed nutrition experts, and others the best that can be formulated on the basis of current knowledge?
- Are nutritionists too cautious in recommending dietary change, or are they recommending change without sufficient research basis?
- Do particular foods threaten the American diet to such an extent that federal guidance and regulations should deviate from their historical approach and treat them as "bad" foods? If so, how should these foods be identified?
- What nutrition messages does the public receive?
- Are these nutrition messages so conflicting that the credibility of the message senders is threatened and public interest in nutrition is lost?

REFERENCES

Block, J. R. 1983. USDA's commitment to nutrition in the 80's. Nutr. Today 18(6):6-12.
Cleveland, L. E., B. B. Peterkin, A. J. Blum, and S. J. Becker. 1983. Recommended dietary allowances as standards for family food plans. J. Nutr. Educ. 15:8-14.
NRC (National Research Council). 1980. Recommended Dietary Allowances, 9th ed. A report

of the Food and Nutrition Board, Assembly of Life Sciences. National Academy of Sciences, Washington, D.C.

Pao, E. M., and S. J. Mickle. 1981. Problem nutrients in the United States. Food Technol. 35(9):58-69.

Peterkin, B. B., and R. L. Rizek. 1984. National nutrition monitoring system. U.S. Department of Agriculture, Agricultural Research Service. Fam. Econ. Rev. 84(4):15-19.

Rizek, R. L., and L. P. Posati. 1985. Continuing survey of food intakes by individuals. U.S. Department of Agriculture, Agricultural Research Service. Fam. Econ. Rev. 85(1):16-17.

USDA (U.S. Department of Agriculture). 1980. Food and Nutrient Intakes of Individuals in 1 Day in the United States, Spring 1977. Nationwide Food Consumption Survey 1977-78. Preliminary Report No. 2. U.S. Department of Agriculture, Washington, D.C. 121 pp.

USDA (U.S. Department of Agriculture). 1984. Directory: Human Nutrition Activities. U.S. Department of Agriculture, Washington, D.C. 21 pp.

USDA and DHHS (U.S. Department of Agriculture and U.S. Department of Health and Human Services). 1980. Nutrition and Your Health: Dietary Guidelines for Americans. HG 232. U.S. Government Printing Office, Washington D.C. 20 pp.

Welsh, S. O., and R. M. Marston. 1982. Zinc levels in U.S. food supply—1909-1980. Food Technol. 36:70-76.

Wolf, J. D., and B. B. Peterkin. 1984. Dietary guidelines: The USDA perspective. Food Technol. 38(7):80-86.

Legal Advocacy for the Hungry and Malnourished: How Can Nutrition Scientists Help?

LYNN PARKER

The Food Research and Action Center (FRAC) is a public interest law firm and advocacy center that works to alleviate hunger and malnutrition in the United States. It provides legal representation, legislative advocacy, policy analysis, research, public education, and training to local organizations that support and monitor federal nutrition programs for low-income Americans. Two of the FRAC's major concerns are the alleviation of hunger and malnutrition in the United States and the quality and adequacy of the federal food assistance programs. Nutrition scientists can assist in these efforts.

DOCUMENTING HUNGER AND MALNUTRITION

Since 1980, FRAC has attempted to convince many policymakers that the combination of recession, unemployment, and some budget decisions have had a negative impact on the ability of many people to obtain an adequate diet. This problem still exists, as reflected in the continuing increase in persons depending on emergency food centers. A recent survey of selected centers showed an average 20% increase in emergency food recipients between 1983 and 1984, with more than 61% of the centers reporting that more than 50% of their clients were families with children (FRAC, 1984).

Although the United States is, on the whole, a wealthy and perhaps overfed nation, 15% of the population lives below the poverty level—a level based on the ability to purchase a minimally nutritious diet (U.S.

Department of Commerce, 1984). Yet, scientists and health professionals have not made the nutritional consequences of that situation clear to policymakers or helped others to document the problem and its consequences in a practical and convincing way.

For example, Edwin Meese, presidential advisor, told the American public in 1983 that many people go to soup kitchens "because the food's free . . . and that's easier than paying for it" (*Washington Post*, 1983). Regarding hungry children, he added, "I've heard a lot of anecdotal stuff, but I haven't heard any authoritative figures." Shortly thereafter, the President's Task Force on Food Assistance—after nationwide hearings and a review of all information the government could gather on the nutritional status of the U.S. population—stated in its final report: "Lack of up-to-date data has made it impossible to assess whether the current nutritional status of the population has worsened over the last years" (President's Task Force on Food Assistance, 1984).

Concerned with this lack of data, 50 health professionals and advocates from around the country recently met under the auspices of FRAC and the University of North Carolina's Child Health Outcomes Project to discuss nutrition monitoring in the 1980s. Models for documenting hunger and malnutrition at the local level were presented. Frustration was expressed at the lack of an inexpensive model for documenting food adequacy problems in a way that would be convincing to local policymakers. I would like to offer nutrition scientists the challenge of helping these health professionals and advocates in their local efforts to document increasing hunger and malnutrition.

IMPROVING THE NUTRITIONAL QUALITY OF CHILD NUTRITION

The National School Lunch Program is a federal food assistance program that provides lunches to 23 million children in the United States every day. When the Department of Health and Human Services is telling the American public that the fat in their diets is probably a controllable contributor to the incidence of cancer, and when so many Americans are struggling to reduce their sodium intake, it makes sense to look more carefully at the meals that are provided to so many schoolchildren every day.

Two recent *Washington Post* (Sugarman, 1984) and *New York Times* (Brody, 1984) articles criticized the nutritional quality of school lunches. The *Times* article quoted a distraught mother: "Everything I do at home is being undermined by the lunch they get at school—hot dogs, hamburgers, cheese, bologna, french fries, fried fish, white bread, fruit canned in heavy syrup, potato chips, whole milk or chocolate milk. Where are the low-fat, low-salt, low-sugar, high-fiber foods [that] experts tell us we should be eating if we want to stay healthy?'' The article also reported on McDonalds' efforts to open their fast-food operations inside schools in competition with school lunch programs.

After describing some of the high-fat, high-salt items being taste-tested by students for local lunch programs, the *Post* article reported: ''Today's food service directors are caught in a bind, a balancing act in which they must juggle economic constraints, parental pressures and the powerful merchandising effects of fast-food restaurants with the need to provide a quick nutritious lunch that students will eat.'' The *Post* further reported that a local high school cafeteria manager claimed to sell 160 servings of french fries and onion rings per day versus 6 individual cartons of yogurt and 35 helpings from the salad bar per day. And, on a questionnaire at a taste party in a local county, students' suggestions for improving the lunch program included adding candy machines, soda machines, and more french fries. Meanwhile, the only program providing funds for nutrition education of schoolchildren, the Nutrition Education and Training Program, has been cut back to $5 million, and since 1980, the administration's yearly budget proposals have eliminated this program, according to the *Post* article.

What is served to children in school obviously reflects what is served to everyone else in homes and restaurants nationwide. However, scientists, academics, health professionals, food industry advisors, and government officials must help local schools to feed children in a more nutritious and healthful way and to teach them lifelong, healthful food habits. This is the second challenge I offer to nutrition scientists.

REFERENCES

Brody, J. E. 1984. Assessing quality of student lunches. New York Times, October 17.

Food Research and Action Center. 1984. Bitter Harvest: A Status Report on the Need for Emergency Food Assistance in America. Food Research and Action Center, Washington, D.C. 68 pp.

President's Task Force on Food Assistance. 1984. Report of the President's Task Force on Food Assistance. Government Printing Office, Washington, D.C. 115 pp.

Sugarman, C. 1984. Testing kids' tastes. Washington Post, October 17.

U.S. Department of Commerce. 1984. Estimates of Poverty Including the Value of Noncash Benefits: 1979 to 1982. A report of the Bureau of the Census. Technical Paper No. 51. U.S. Department of Commerce, Washington, D.C. 172 pp.

Washington Post. 1983. Meese: ''The food is free and...that's easier than paying for it.'' December 10.

Participants and Coauthors

DAVID M. BOUSH, Doctoral Student, Department of Marketing and Business Law, University of Minnesota, Minneapolis, Minnesota

JOHANNA DWYER, Director, Frances Stern Nutrition Center, New England Medical Center Hospital, Boston, Massachusetts

APRIL FALLON, Assistant Professor of Psychology, Department of Psychiatry, Medical College of Pennsylvania, Philadelphia, Pennsylvania

BASILE GOUNGETAS, Research Associate, Department of Agricultural Economics, University of Missouri, Columbia, Missouri

HELEN GUTHRIE, Professor, Department of Nutrition, Pennsylvania State University, University Park, Pennsylvania

JEAN-PIERRE HABICHT, James Jamison Professor of Nutritional Epidemiology, Division of Nutritional Sciences, Cornell University, Ithaca, New York

CLIFFORD JOHNSON, Chief, Nutrition Statistics Branch, Division of Health Examination Statistics, National Center for Health Statistics, Hyattsville, Maryland

STANLEY JOHNSON, Professor, The Center for Agricultural and Rural Development, Iowa State University, Des Moines, Iowa

GILBERT LEVEILLE, Director, Nutrition and Health Sciences, Division of Central Research, General Foods Corporation, White Plains, New York

165

KAREN J. MORGAN, Associate Professor, Department of Human
   Nutrition, Foods and Food Systems Management, University of
   Missouri, Columbia, Missouri
ROBERT MURPHY, Director, Division of Health Examination Statistics,
   National Center for Health Statistics, Hyattsville, Maryland
LYNN PARKER, Nutritionist, Food Research and Action Center,
   Washington, D.C.
BETTY B. PETERKIN, Deputy Center Director, Consumer Nutrition
   Center, Human Nutrition Information Service, U.S. Department of
   Agriculture, Hyattsville, Maryland
KENNETH ROERING, Chairman, Department of Marketing, School of
   Management, University of Minnesota, Minneapolis, Minnesota
PAUL ROZIN, Professor, Department of Psychology, University of
   Pennsylvania, Philadelphia, Pennsylvania
BENJAMIN SENAUER, Associate Professor of Applied Economics,
   Department of Agriculture and Applied Economics, University of
   Minnesota, St. Paul, Minnesota
SHANNON H. SHIPP, Doctoral Student, Department of Marketing and
   Business Law, University of Minnesota, Minneapolis, Minnesota
JAMES KREBS-SMITH, Instructor, Department of Nutrition,
   Pennsylvania State University, University Park, Pennsylvania
SUSAN M. KREBS-SMITH, Doctoral Student, Department of Nutrition,
   Pennsylvania State University, University Park, Pennsylvania
SUSAN WELSH, Division Director, Nutrition Education Division, U.S.
   Department of Agriculture, Hyattsville, Maryland
CATHERINE WOTEKI, Deputy Director, Division of Health Examination
   Statistics, National Center for Health Statistics, Hyattsville,
   Maryland
HELEN SMICIKLAS-WRIGHT, Associate Professor, Department of
   Nutrition, Pennsylvania State University, University Park,
   Pennsylvania

Index

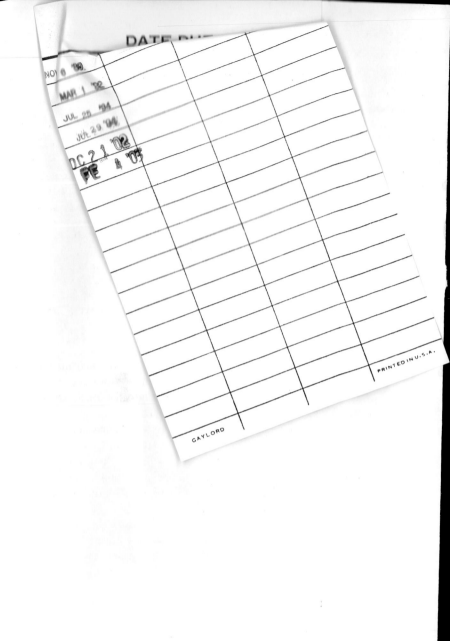